The Sound of God's Voice Singing

GOD'S INVITATIONS TO WALK
IN THE LIGHT THROUGH A WORLD
OF DARKNESS

James A Kitchens, PhD

"God is light; in him there is no darkness at all." (1 John 1:5)

TRILOGY CHRISTIAN PUBLISHERS
TUSTIN, CA

TRILOGY

Trilogy Christian Publishers

A Wholly Owned Subsidiary of Trinity Broadcasting Network

2442 Michelle Drive

Tustin, CA 92780

Guardians of the Twelve: Jacob and the Lion Pendant

Copyright © 2024 by James A. Kitchens, PhD

Unless noted otherwise, scripture quotations are taken from the Holy Bible, New International Version®, NIV®. Copyright © 1985 by Biblica, Inc.™ Used by permission of Zondervan. All rights reserved worldwide. www.zondervan.com. The "NIV" and "New International Version" are trademarks registered in the United States Patent and Trademark Office by Biblica, Inc.™.

Scripture quotations marked "BLB" are taken from The Holy Bible, Berean Literal Bible, BLB. Copyright ©2016, 2018 by Bible Hub. Used by Permission. All Rights Reserved Worldwide. www.berean.bible.

Scripture quotations marked "BSB" are taken from The Holy Bible, Berean Study Bible, BSB. Copyright ©2016, 2018 by Bible Hub. Used by Permission. All Rights Reserved Worldwide. www.berean.bible. Scripture quotations marked CEV are taken from the Contemporary English Version®. Copyright © 1995 American Bible Society. All rights reserved.

Scripture quotations marked CSB are taken from the Christian Standard Bible®, Copyright © 2017 by Holman Bible Publishers. Used by permission. Christian Standard Bible, and CSB®, are federally registered trademarks of Holman Bible Publishers.

Scripture quotations marked EHV are from the Holy Bible, Evangelical Heritage Version® (EHV®) © 2019 Wartburg Project, Inc. All rights reserved.

Scripture quotations marked ESV are taken from the ESV® Bible (The Holy Bible, English Standard Version®), copyright © 2001 by Crossway Bibles, a publishing ministry of Good News Publishers. Used by permission. All rights reserved.

Scripture quotations marked GNT are taken from the Good News Translation® (Today's English Version, Second Edition). Copyright © 1982 American Bible Society. All rights reserved.

Scripture quotations marked ISV are taken from the Holy Bible: International Standard Version® Copyright © 1996-2013 by the ISV Foundation. Used by permission of Davidson Press, LLC. All rights reserved internationally.

Scripture quotations marked NASB are taken from the New American Standard Bible® (NASB), Copyright © 1960, 1962, 1963, 1968, 1971, 1972, 1973, 1975, 1977, 1995 by The Lockman Foundation. Used by permission. www.Lockman.org.

Scripture quotations marked NLT are taken from the Holy Bible, New Living Translation, copyright © 1996, 2004, 2015 by Tyndale House Foundation. Used by permission of Tyndale House Publishers, Inc., Carol Stream, Illinois 60188. All rights reserved.

Scripture quotations marked (NRSV) are taken from the New Revised Standard Version Bible, copyright © 1989 National Council of the Churches of Christ in the United States of America. Used by permission. All rights reserved. Scripture quotations marked KJV are taken from the King James Version of the Bible. Public domain.

All rights reserved, including the right to reproduce this book or portions thereof in any form whatsoever.

For information, address Trilogy Christian Publishing

Rights Department, 2442 Michelle Drive, Tustin, Ca 92780.

Trilogy Christian Publishing/ TBN and colophon are trademarks of Trinity Broadcasting Network.

For information about special discounts for bulk purchases, please contact Trilogy Christian Publishing.

Trilogy Disclaimer: The views and content expressed in this book are those of the author and may not necessarily reflect the views and doctrine of Trilogy Christian Publishing or the Trinity Broadcasting Network.

10 9 8 7 6 5 4 3 2 1

Library of Congress Cataloging-in-Publication Data is available.

ISBN 979-8-89041-798-5

ISBN 979-8-89041-799-2 (e-book)

*For Aubrey Jean.
She came to us and won our hearts,
truly a song God is singing.*

Acknowledgments

It all started with *Sweet Pea*, and my mom was mostly responsible for that. My father was a blue-collar carpenter, and we lived in low-income housing in Biloxi, Mississippi. When I was in the seventh grade, we moved to the piney woods of rural Louisiana. We were poor, but we were church folks. Church found us there twice on Sunday and every Wednesday night, without fail. But most importantly, my mom read to me and bought me books, and my dad especially was a great storyteller. I loved stories: fiction, biblical, and true-life stories from my extended family. Nothing made me happier than sitting around the supper table and listening to my dad telling stories from his growing-up years. I didn't do so well with numbers, but words were my delight.

And that is where *Sweet Pea* came in. I began my first book, a novel, when I was in the fourth grade. On the first page of a new tablet, I wrote the words, "Sweet Pea came running over the hill." I can still see the picture that was in my mind. I saw a beautiful gray mare in a pasture filled with tall grass and wildflowers, with a meandering stream in the background. I never wrote a second sentence, but I was hooked. From that moment on, I knew I was to be a writer.

So, I begin this book with gratitude to that gray horse, to all the horses I have loved over the years, and to my mom and dad for the encouragement and inspiration they were to a growing boy and to the man he became. I say thank you to my teachers, including Sunday School teachers, who guided me from the beginning all the way through graduate school. We are, each of us, but the culmination of our teachers, combined with the gifts which God has implanted in us. I number among my teachers, my two children and their mates, and my grandson and his wife. I thank them for all they taught me as I watched them grow up and for what I see now as they live their lives as contributing adults.

I thank my friends at First Baptist Church, Nacogdoches, Texas, and the members of the Men's Sunday Morning Bible Study, of which I have served as a teacher for the last several years. We have discussed much of what is written on these pages, and their attentive presence and feedback have impacted my thinking greatly. Their friendship and the inspiration of their lives and character have been a constant encouragement to me.

I am especially grateful for the excellent help of the Trilogy Christian Publishing editorial staff. The quality of the final product of this book owes much to their gentile suggestions for changes and improvements. I also must thank Brad Patton, among this group, for guiding me safely through the maze of getting this process started.

And a special word of gratitude to Rachel, my wife of over fifty years, for her strength, wisdom, deep faith in God, and gentle love. None of this would have been possible without her, nor, to tell the truth, would it have been nearly as much fun. She has offered encouragement, inspiration, guidance, insight, and laughter across the years. My prayer is that I might be a man worthy of her love.

Jim Kitchens
Nacogdoches, Texas

Contents

INTRODUCTION xii

CHAPTER 1: THE PATH OF LOVE 1
    As You Love Yourself 1
    What Made God Do It? 5
    When I Say "I Love You," What Do I Mean? 9
    The Joy and the Pain of Love 13
    Thinking About God Thinking About Me 17
    Do You Know the Word "Pusillanimity"? 22
    The Fifth Sparrow 26

CHAPTER 2: THE PATH OF FAITH 31
    On Caterpillars and Butterflies 31
    When Climbing, Take Little Steps 35
    What Ever Happened to Sin? 39
    Faith Conquers Fear... 43
    An Ant of Extraordinary Valor 49
    Mustard Seed Faith 53

CHAPTER 3: THE PATH OF HOPE 58
    Our God Is Marching On 58
    Wonder and a Wooden Post... 65
    The Tyranny of Freedom 69
    Does God Have a Funny Bone? 73
    The Thread 78

The Day Jeremiah Bought the Brooklyn Bridge 82

On Being a Pilgrim and Sojourner 86

CHAPTER 4: THE PATH OF MIRACLES AND UNEXPECTED BLESSINGS 91

The Finger of God 92

Fifty-Two Years of Wedding Bells 96

The Star of Bethlehem 99

Does the Bush Still Burn? 105

Everything Is a Gift 108

Believe Until You Receieve 112

The Sound of God's Voice Singing 116

CHAPTER 5: WALKING TO SERVE 121

To Whom Has God Given You? 122

What Are We Doing to Our Children? 126

Do You Wait Well? 130

In Part 133

Little Things 137

The Judas Heart 141

CHAPTER 6: GOD'S HELP ALONG THE WAY 145

Just When We Need Him Most 145

Dancing on the Edge of a Volcano 149

God, What Do We Do When the Brook Runs Dry? ... 154

What Is a Blessing? 158

All Have Sinned 162

I Love to Tell the Story 165

CHAPTER 7: THE BEAUTIES AND WONDERS OF THE
   WAY 170
   Heading Home 170
   Sunday All Week Long 174
   Longing for God... 178
   Living Easter Every Day.................................... 182
   The Positive Effects of Failure 187
   Finding Philadelphia 190
   Why Pray? 194
CHAPTER 8: NEARING THE DESTINATION 199
   The Land Beyond Imagination 200
   A Living Hope for "Old-Timers" 204
   How to Get Down from a Desk 208
   But If He Does Not 211
   Praying Is Dangerous...................................... 215
   The Race Track 219
EPILOGUE: THE SHIP 225

Introduction

"You are the light of the world…. Let your light shine that men may see…" (Matthew 5:14; 5:16).

There is a cave about halfway between Fort Worth and Houston on Interstate 45 called Inner Space. Once, when my children were small, my son about six and my daughter about three, I stopped there with them to visit the cave. The cave guide took a group of about twenty people into the cave and explained what we were looking at as we went. Electric lights illuminated the way along a concrete pathway bounded by a metal handrail to guide us.

Occasionally, there was a concrete wall on which a life-size picture of a prehistoric animal had been painted. In one place, a twenty-foot tusk of a giant wooly mammoth (elephant) had been unearthed. At another place, there was a small cavern about the size of half a football field and thirty or forty feet deep. It was lighted, and we could see the bones of animals that had wandered into the cave and fell into that hole. They died there because they could not get out. I shuttered at their fate.

After about forty-five minutes and about a quarter of a mile distance, the cave guide explained that he was going to turn the lights off for about thirty seconds to give us a sense of what real darkness is like. He asked that we stay silent until the lights were turned on again. That was the longest thirty seconds in my life. My son was at my left side and was holding my left hand with a death grip. I was holding my daughter in my right arm, and I felt her arms tighten about my neck.

When the light went off, I noticed immediately that I lost all sense of equilibrium. I had no sense of up or down, right or left, big or little. I was totally lost in every sense of that word. I had no use of any of my senses. My whole being was relieved when the lights came back on. It was as if I had come alive again. I enjoyed the cave overall and learned a lot. But I was glad to get back into Texas' sunlight.

I was reminded of that experience recently when I was reading Jesus' words in the Sermon on the Mount when He declared that His followers are "light" in a world of darkness (Matthew 5:14). In a sense, this statement is among the most complimentary things which Jesus can say about us disciples. After all, He said elsewhere, "As long as I am in the world, I am the light of the world" (John 9:5, ESV). When He commanded His followers to be the light of the world, He demanded that we be nothing less than like Him!

Physical light is a necessity for life itself. That is why light was the first thing that God spoke into existence (Genesis 1:3). Light is our primary tool for perceiving the world. We do not see light; we use light to see the world around us. Yet sunlight does much more than help us to see.

Our light begins in the sun, ninety-three million miles away. It takes about eight minutes for the light originating in the fires of the sun to reach Earth. That light is energy that warms the earth to the perfect temperature to support life. It drives global weather patterns and initiates the life-sustaining process called photosynthesis. Light provides a window into the universe, supports our perception of spatial relationships, and gives markers, allowing us to sense the passing of time. Everything we enjoy about life as we know it would be impossible without God's amazing gift of light.

When Jesus spoke of the "light of the world," He was using the sun's light as a metaphor for a totally different kind of light. He was speaking of spiritual light, which is even more necessary than physical light. Jesus Himself is the source of that light. When He walked on earth as a human among humans, He announced Himself to be the "light of the world" (John 8:12). To understand what He meant by this statement, imagine a lighthouse on a stormy night giving guidance to a ship in tumultuous and dangerous waters. Paul had that concept in mind when he wrote, "For God, who said, 'Let light shine out of darkness,' made his light shine in our hearts to give us light of the knowledge of the glory of God in the face of Christ" (2 Corinthians 4:6, ESV).

Jesus is the source of the light that shines through believers. He remains the "light of the world," but now He shines that light through His followers. Jesus in us is the light that shines from our life. He directs us like that lighthouse guides a helpless ship. He is our guide; He is the equilibrium, the steadiness, the balance that not only enables us to see the pathway but the strength to walk that path. As Psalm 119:105 (ESV) says, "Your word is a lamp to my feet and a light to my path." He provides a lighted path through a world of darkness. Indeed, He is even the source of the *desire* to walk His trail.

Jesus means that Christianity is something that is to be seen. One cannot be a secret disciple. As He said, we are a "city set on a hill" (Matthew 5:14, NASB). Our light must be seen in the ordinary activities of the world. It must be visible in how we treat the checkout person at the grocery store, the person behind us in line, or a fellow worker at our job. The light should shine in our treatment of our waitress, how we drive or park our car, our politeness and courtesy to members of our family, and our kindness to the animals with which we interact. No area of our ordinary, everyday life is exempt.

I recall reading about an elementary teacher who said that she tried every time she had to correct a child to do it with her arm around that child. I have often counseled people, when dealing with a controversial topic with a spouse or child, to try to do so while having a hand on the arm or shoulder of the other person. It is well, as we think about being light, to remember the sage advice of that wise philosopher Oprah Winfree. Paraphrasing Maya Angelou, she said, "People seldom remember what you say or do. But they never forget how you make them feel."

The light to which Jesus calls us enables others to see our "good works." That is, the light is our changed life. The word Jesus used for "good" describes a thing that is not only "good" in quality but is also captivating, beautiful, and attractive. There is charm in these works. They are lovely and contain no element of hardness, coldness, or unconcern. They are not pushy, judgmental, or disdainful.

Jesus also intends that we be motivated by drawing attention, not to ourselves, but to God. There is no "theatrical goodness" here. No boastful posturing to gain accolades for ourselves. As Paul reminded us, we cannot boast about our "good works" because we are "God's masterpiece. He has created us anew in Christ Jesus, so we can do the good things he planned for us long ago" (Ephesians 2:10, NLT). We shine so that people will glorify God and be drawn to Him.

Our light is always a borrowed light. We are like moonlight. The moon has no light in itself. What we see when we experience moonlight is reflected light that has its origin in the sun. In ourselves, we can never kindle the light that provides the balance we experience as we take each step. Jesus is the inner light that differentiates between the right and the wrong, the left and the right, the up and the down. He gives the sense that we are moving in the right direction, that we are following a way of safety in a world of pitfalls into which we can fall and never escape. The radiance that shines from us is Jesus alive in our hearts. He is the light that shines in our life.

Recently, I was reading a book by James Finley about Thomas Merton, who was a Trappist monk and lived at Gethsemane Monastery in Kentucky. He was a prolific writer of exceptional books on spiritual topics who has had a great influence on my faith. Finley said this about him. "Merton was and is no more than a window through whom we may perhaps catch a glimpse of the One who had called him to a life of prayer and solitude." This is an awesome description of all Christians, you and me included. We are no more than a window through whom flows the light that overcomes the darkness. Through us shines a light which is a guide to God.

These writings you are about to read are like love letters from God to His children. They are letters from home. It was my fingers that touched the keyboard, but it was God using me as a musician who uses a saxophone to make marvelous music. They are like shafts of light in the darkness of this world. And this world is dark. Bombs fall in Ukraine and Israel, China makes friends with our allies in the Mideast, inflation drives the cost of energy and food through the roof, the media and the corporate world push woke madness, political corruption sits at the highest level of our government, the Supreme Court redefines marriage as family life falls apart, Critical Race Theory drives a wedge of hatred between black and white people, diversity offices instruct us to be ashamed of our country and its values, and the academic world tells us either that there is no God or if there is, He does not matter. We desperately need light in this tsunami of darkness.

The goal of this book is not to provide an immediate, practical guide to action designed to solve these problems. This is not a book of six easy steps to being a light in the world. It is not designed to give advice or to draw up a line of action. The goal is tougher and goes deeper than that. The objective is to make you think. It is to probe, to question, to raise issues in the reader's life that are in need of transformation. This book seeks to "throw a little light" on open avenues to God's powerful presence in the breathtaking task of being a Christian in a dark world. What we need is God in our lives. These writings are God's love letters asking us to let Him in and telling us what to expect if we do.

Each section of each chapter is designed to challenge and inform you. And each section, as well as each chapter, can stand alone. Therefore, it is not necessary to begin at the beginning and read through to the end. You may read and reread at any place that interests you and in whatever order you wish.

The Christian life is a long and often arduous journey, during which we are increasingly opened up to a growing new self, to a way of life for which we were originally intended, and to the light of God's life living out in us. The old country-western song has it, "I Saw the Light." Yes, we can see the light, and the light will see us, and we will become God's light in a world of darkness.

• CHAPTER 1 •

The Path of Love

Many years ago, I bought a book on horsemanship from a professional horse trainer named Jonnie Stinson. When the book arrived, I discovered that she had personally inscribed the flyleaf with some simple lines. It read:

My motto:
Love is the method, and love is the reward.
Jonnie Stinson

Actually, Jesus could autograph His story with the same words. He uses His love both as a method to teach us how to walk the way to which He calls us and also as our reward for walking that way. It is that very same love.

As You Love Yourself

"If you do not know how to love yourself, you cannot truthfully love your neighbor."

Augustine of Hippo

Every morning, for about three years, when I was in high school, I was a milk delivery man. An elderly couple who were shut-ins, Mr. and Mrs. Hudson, lived about a half mile down the gravel road from our house. After I had milked the cows and done my other morning chores, I carried two quarts of milk, free of charge, to them. I placed the bottles of fresh milk on their porch and picked up the two empty bottles that awaited me. I did this because I was a Christian, and Jesus encouraged His followers to love others. He was a great example for me on how to care about people who are especially needy.

To my knowledge, Mr. and Mrs. Hudson, since they didn't see me, never thanked me for my daily gift. I can't remember my parents or anybody else ever acknowledging my kindness or thoughtfulness. In fact, no one but my parents ever knew what I did. I may have mentioned this experience once or twice as a classroom illustration of some sort or other, but I never got any public recognition for my deeds. Yet, I remember the extreme joy I felt each time I made my way home with those empty milk bottles. I think I often skipped for joy.

Love and loving acts make us joyful. We Christians have repeatedly heard it said that love is a gift from God that is rewarded with happiness. We desire love for the joy that it brings us. It is good not only for our soul, but love benefits our physical body with greater health and longer life. Love is good for us in every way. That being the case, would it not follow that all love then is no more than a self-centered act which is, no matter how rationalized, merely a form of self-love? The answer to that question is yes, and it is okay! That truth about love does not make love a negative act. God made love that way because it is the only way that love can work.

As a matter of fact, all basic acts of self-care take place by nature. That is, they are instinctive and do not have to be learned. It comes naturally for us to jerk our fingers away from a hot stove. When we are thirsty, we do not need to be taught to seek water to satisfy that thirst. Even the tiniest infant cries out when she wants something to relieve the pain of hunger. God created us with the urge to seek the fulfillment of our needs. All acts of "self-preservation," as they are called, come naturally. They are part of us because we are human. It is not too much to say that the craving to love and be loved falls in that same category.

The functioning of our natural hunger for love is a part of our desire for a full or meaningful life. All normal human beings seek comfort, joy, bliss, and happiness. We cannot deny, divert, or dismiss these longings and remain human. They dominate all our feelings and conscious decisions. Of course, we do have the capacity to "defer gratification" in the short run to achieve a greater reward in the long run. I may, as an example, stay home to study on a Friday night rather than party with my friends in order to achieve the joy of a higher score on Saturday's examination. But my goal is always my sense of satisfaction and happiness.

It is not a bit surprising or, in the least, degrading to realize that we love others and seek their love because we desire personal happiness. No, it is not. That is why Jesus could say that the second greatest commandment is, "You shalt love your neighbor as you love yourself" (Matthew 22:39). Jesus is saying, it seems to me, that the love by which we love ourselves must be the standard we use to measure our love for others.

How is that possible? Can it be that the naturalness by which I care for and watch over myself becomes the naturalness by which I care for and watch over others? Sigmund Freud, one of the founders of psychology, once wrote that Jesus' command to love others, especially our enemies, is "foolish nonsense." Love, he said, is far too precious to be "spread promiscuously around." It is to be saved for and savored by the special few in our life. I disagree.

I make allowances for myself. Josef Pieper, a German philosopher from the last century who was a Christian, put it well. He said that each person automatically has the opinion, "It is good that I exist." I am at least somewhat aware of my faults, my weaknesses, and my failures. In most cases, despite these liabilities, in general, I still give myself overall approval. C. S. Lewis commented that he was always uneasy with the saying, "Hate the sin, and love the sinner." Then, one day, he realized that there was one person in the world toward whom he had followed that precept all his life. That person was himself.

Let me go back to that teenager in South Louisiana carrying milk to an elderly couple. I have carefully considered this experience of loving care. To be absolutely honest, I must admit that I wanted the joy and happiness that accompanied my gift of love to the Hudsons. I "approved of myself," and that was an exceedingly pleasant part of the experience. I was also aware that anyone who might become aware of what I did every morning before catching the bus to school would be impressed with and approve of me. I very much enjoyed that image in my mind. I know that I also wanted to help others. But I seriously doubt that the desire to help others came first, and the joy and sense of satisfaction as a rich reward came later.

Looking back years after this event, I realize that God was using my natural desire for happiness and joy to do something much greater than making a teenager happy. God was forging my character. He was building a philosophy of life, a way of seeing my place in the world and how I would live my life. I was actually experiencing a truth clearly presented in the Scriptures. Helping others by giving your life in service to those who are needy makes one happy.

God blesses in numerous ways those who are aware of the needs of others and seek a way to encourage, inspire, and assist them along the way. He calls each of His children, regardless of their vocation or station in life, to that outlook. It starts within our family and extends to our neighborhood, to our workplace, and to groups to which we belong. We want that blessing, and we want that blessing for others. That is the second greatest commandment. *Love others as you love yourself!*

What Made God Do It?

"In the beginning, God created…" (Genesis 1:1).

I suppose that most human beings have stood in awe before the grandeur of creation. And the more science demonstrates the complexities of the cosmos, the more we see not only the creativity of God but also His imaginative power and engineering skill. Truly, "The heavens declare the glory of God" (Ps 19:1). But I think there is an even greater and more mysterious factor in contemplating creation. That is the question, "What made God do it?" That is, "What quality in God motivated to bring the universe into being?"

At first glance, it would seem that God had no good reason to do what He did. He is infinite and perfect in every way. He needs nothing outside Himself to complete Him. Since He needs nothing, there is no way that He could benefit from creating this beautiful cosmos and the billions of beings who inhabit it. What moved Him to do it?

The truth, of course, is that no one can answer that because of two simple reasons:

1) No human can *know* the mind of God. Indeed, no human being can know the mind even of another human, much less the mind of God. Yet we try. It seems that asking "why" is a part of human nature and, in itself, is a good thing. We have made many wonderful discoveries out of our need to find the answer to the question "why." But to fathom the mind of another person or God is beyond our capabilities.

Even if we could enter the mind of God, human language [is] too weak and limited to explain what we would find there. [We are co]nfined to metaphors derived from human behavior [to describe] God. We say He is a father, a shepherd, a shield, a [fortress,] a lion, a lamb, a door, a still small voice, a rock. [We use all sorts] of human traits to describe him. He comforts, [He forg]ives, He perseveres, He keeps His promises, [etc. A]s we approach the question of why God [created, we must] begin by admitting that we can offer no [definitive answer. We] search, nonetheless, for an answer. ["To be or n]ot to be; that is the question."¹ Nor [do we kno]w the answer to that question. To

¹ [The Comple]te Works of William Shakespeare. Act

be, to have life, is better than not to be. When God created, He not only made things, He gave life. He is life; He gave life, and life is God's greatest gift. And, as noted, He did so without the possibility of receiving any benefit for Himself.

We use the word "generous" to describe such a gift. In fact, you may call His gift of life the zenith of generosity. God's generosity in His creative act is in a class by itself. No other gift in all the world is similar to God's gift of life. It is the absolute gift *because* He could reap no personal benefit from the giving *and because* the ones receiving the gift (you and me) are a part of the gift itself.

Because I am a human being, I can never give like that. But let me tell you of a gift that my wife Rachel and I gave years ago that comes as close as we could ever come to giving like that. Over a period of years, we gave a large sum of money to a needy family that lived near us. We were not related to them, and I can no longer even remember their names or how many children they had. We made sure that no one would ever know that we were the givers. (I can't tell you any more than that because then someone would know what we did.)

You might say that we got nothing from giving that gift. But you would be wrong. We got a deep sense of satisfaction from that deed, which, to tell the truth, is better than any recognition or accolade we could have received. We still return, years later, to the sweet memory of that gift (without smugness or undue pride, we pray). Our gift to that family was also a gift to ourselves, a gift that keeps on giving.

If God got nothing, why did He do it? Here is a partial answer. Everything God does reveals who He is. I do not know if God created everything in order to reveal Himself. I only know that we do know Him by what He has done. His creation not only shows His intelligent creativity and imagination, but it also reveals that He is magnanimous (unselfish, gracious), munificent (bestows lavish benefits), and benevolent (kindhearted, warmhearted, and well-meaning). No wonder that the Bible says simply, "God is love" (1 John 4:8).

From His very first act, God demonstrated His grace, His compassion, and His desire to give wonderous and miraculous gifts. Should we be surprised that Paul said that God would bring good from everything (Romans 8:28)? How could we doubt that God has a design for each of us, "plans to prosper you and not to harm you, plans to give you hope and a future" (Jeremiah 29:11)? Thus, God's creation makes a statement about each of us. God created each person, and that means that each of us is the recipient of God's super generosity and benevolence. We live because God wanted us to. Each one is the product of God's careful plan and design. No one is an accident.

The atheists say that humans and everything else are the product of blind chance that had no direction or design in mind. Everything is an accidental outcome of evolutionary development.

Space does not allow me the opportunity to show the logical as well as the biological impossibilities so apparent in their theories. The simple fact is that a designer is necessary in so dazzling a design. And God fits the bill. He is hidden in plain sight in the wonder of His creation. In creation, He reveals not only His power but His grace and compassion.

We live today between earth and sky. When we see our habitat as a gift from God, a miracle occurs. The awareness of that gift becomes an awareness of God. We awaken as we begin to know Him (not know about Him). That, I think, is His motive. Do not misunderstand. It is not that He needed or wanted to be known. Rather, He knew that human beings, the highest of His creation, would be created with the need to know Him. So, out of His love, He made that possible. Thus, we awaken to Him like the coming of the dawn. Slowly, over time, not as a blinding flash. And when we ask, "Why, God?" He answers in love, "Come, follow me."

When I Say "I Love You," What Do I Mean?

Josef Pieper (1904–1997) is considered one of the great German philosophers of the last century. He was also a committed Christian. He published his first book, *On Courage*, in 1934. Hitler and his Nazi perspective were on the rise in Germany, and Pieper could see the handwriting on the wall. He knew that it would take enormous strength and courage for Christians to stand against the ungodly system that Hitler brought to Germany. Pieper noted that the book was an angry appeal for the courage to rebel in the face of evil.

The editor at the company that published his book commissioned him to write a book on love. Pieper wrestled for years to write an acceptable book on this subject. However, nothing he wrote satisfied him. It was not until 1974 (forty years later), after the publication of a number of other well-received books, that he published his book on love.

Pieper explained his dilemma. The single word "love" is used to cover a multitude of human activities. It is a verb describing something we do or practice. It is also a noun describing some powerful and often sudden experience that comes over us, like an enchantment or fascination. It covers feelings directed toward possessing and enjoying.

On the other hand, love may refer to a self-forgetful gesture. It can be both desire and giving at one and the same time. It may describe a turning toward someone, even God, or simply turning to a stranger needing our help. It may describe our enjoyment of something like sports or a drink. It is used to depict some act of God or even the deepest quality of God's character—"God is love" (1 John 4:8).

For Pieper, it seemed improbable that such diverse uses of a single word could be supported by any kind of common element. Would it not be impossible to answer the question, "What is love??" We can assume that love is something good, but what exactly that good is remains a mystery.

However, Pieper reasoned that love, so widely used, must describe some actual human experience. Love, whatever it is, is real. There must be some "lowest common denominator" to borrow a term from the world of mathematics. Can we find it? He says, "In every conceivable case love signifies much the same as approval…. Loving someone or something means finding him or it [...] 'good.' It is a way of saying [...] 'It's good that you exist.'"

Notice how God expressed His approval in Genesis by His affirmation at the conclusion of each day's creation, "It is good." On day six, when He brought human beings into existence, His comment was, "It is very good" (Genesis 1:31). God's love is as if He is saying, "I want you to be. My desire is that you exist." Consider the profane statement, "God damn you." Here is an expression of love's polar opposite. This comment is actually a prayer that God would destroy the existence of a person or thing.

Every normal human being, from the earliest age to his last days, desperately longs for two fundamental things: we want to be seen, and we want the seer to like what he sees. There is a natural desire in each of us for approval. Little children announce it openly. They say, "Look at me!" And they want us to look and then give an approving word. Not only so, but psychological well-being and proper adjustment in life make that approval necessary. I have frequently said to my students and others that if you want to give love to others, look at them by asking questions about what is happening in their lives and find in their answers places where you can truthfully offer approval. That is what loving is all about.

God wants us to exist. The Psalms are filled with affirmations of God's desire for our existence. Psalm 139 is a beautiful example. "You created my inmost being; you knit me together in my mother's womb. I praise you because I am fearfully and wonderfully made" (Psalm 139:13–14). Psalm 18:19 is another example: "He brought me out into a spacious place; he rescued me because he delights in me." The rabbis interpret the first part of this verse as a reference to birth. He brought us from the womb into the world, and He did it because He delights in us. He loves us and wants us to exist. He says by the very fact of our life that it is good for us to be here.

How do we explain God's delight that we exist? I think I saw it on a bus ride one summer in Jerusalem. Public transportation buses have one spot over the front wheels where seats face toward the back. Riders in those seats sit face to face, or knee to knee, with riders across from them. The buses are always loud and crowded with people standing in the aisle. One morning, on my way to work, a young Jewish woman sat across from me with an infant lying in the depression between her thighs. I assumed she was the baby's mother.

For the entirety of the ride, lasting about thirty minutes, that young woman did not take her eyes off that baby. She cooed, kissed, smiled, and said soft words to that child. Her eyes were shining with loving pride. I watched as she "delighted" in that baby. Her every move was designed to say, in Pieper's words, "I approve of you; it is good that you exist." Good, perhaps, is not sufficient. It is very good, exceptionally good that you exist. It is not good that you are clever, smart, talented, rich, beautiful, and famous. No, it is good that you are. It is wonderful that you are. That is a description of God's delight that each of us exists.

We must, I think, add one other element to Pieper's perspective on love. When we are talking about loving another person, not only does love mean that I am glad you exist, but it offers itself in help and encouragement to fulfill that existence. When love sees another, love sees a work in progress, a potential on the way to fulfillment. That is why I could tell my students, strangers whom I knew for only a little while, that I loved them. Each had a right to existence, and I would help them within the proper professional boundaries to fulfill the potential of that existence.

I love my wife, children, my friends, strangers, and even my enemies with that same love. And I love myself like that also. I must admit, however, that my love for my wife and my love for a stranger in need differs in both depth and duration. Despite these differences, it remains the same basic quality. Love is there saying, "It is good that you exist."

And God? Does this concept work as we fulfill the greatest commandment? Yes, with a proviso. I can truly say to God, "I am glad you exist!" Remember, God's name is "I am," "I exist," "I am being." In my love for God, I offer my "help." I will give myself to show gratitude, bring glory to His name, and help Him to be known. I can truly say to God, "I love you," and exactly know what I am saying!

The Joy and the Pain of Love

"Out of love comes joy as well as sadness."
Thomas Aquinas

Human beings instinctively seek love. All normal human beings are naturally equipped at birth to seek love and to give love. The process of growth and maturation in the first few years of life develops the extent and the manner of expression of that natural trait. The necessity of love in those early years has been demonstrated by a multitude of scientific studies since early in the last century. It is a well-established fact that receiving love in the first three or four years of life is absolutely necessary for psychological well-being in the adult years.

What is more, we continue throughout life to seek love because love makes us happy. Indeed, it may be said that all real human happiness is the happiness of love. There may be a fleeting happiness that comes with accomplishment, promotion, or financial success. One may have a justified and well-deserved sense of pride when "my team wins." These going-ons, however, are like jumping hurdles. You are elated when you clear one, but immediately, your eyes are on the next one you must jump.

It turns out that only genuine, legitimate love can bring long-lasting, even life-long, joy. Whether it is directed toward or received from a spouse, a son, a daughter, a friend, a pet, or God Himself, only that love can produce real happiness. There are, of course, countless things that will bring deep, real joy. But they are all based on a common experience. They make us happy because we receive from or give to something or someone we love.

Many scholars have pointed out, and I think correctly, that an individual who loves nothing or no one cannot himself truly rejoice or find long-lasting happiness. We find evidence of the truth of that statement by considering love's opposite. The opposite of love is not hate but indifference. Indifference is the "despairing conclusion that nothing matters." It is the attitude that says, "I don't give a damn because nothing, including me, is important" (Or worse, nothing *except* me is important.) One Russian novelist of the last century has a character ask the question, "What is hell?" After a moment of silence, he answers his own question, "I maintain that it is the inability to love." He continues to think aloud and describes humans as "spiritual creatures" placed in time and space who, on coming to earth, are given the awesome power to say, "I am, and I love!"

But there is another side to love. Love has the power to make us unhappy. Sigmund Freud, an early founder of the discipline of psychology, said, "Never are we less protected against suffering than when we love." Love lays bare one's soul in ultimate vulnerability. This truth is as old as the biblical story of Jacob's impassioned love for Rachel. He agreed with Laban, Rachel's father, to work for seven years for her, only to be duped by Laban, who substituted Leah, his oldest daughter, on the wedding day. Jacob agreed to work another seven years because of his love for Rachel.

Shakespeare's plays are filled with stories of the pain of unfulfilled love. Remember Romeo and Juliette? Or consider the inimitable words of C. S. Lewis on this subject: "Love anything and your heart will certainly be wrung and possibly be broken. If you want to make sure of keeping it intact, you must give your heart to no one, not even to an animal."

Lewis knew whereof he spoke on this subject. In 1956, as a confirmed bachelor, he married Joy Davidman, a divorced American citizen. He was forty-six years old. Because of the enmity of her former husband, she did not wish to return to the US from England, but her visa was about to expire. Lewis agreed to a marriage of convenience to help her remain in England. What they were unprepared for was that they fell in love. But Joy died four short years later in 1960 from cancer, and Lewis was left alone with a broken heart. Lewis experienced the immense cost of true love.

If, as many acknowledge, love means to rejoice in the happiness of another, does it not follow that love also means to feel the sadness and the unhappiness of another? As Paul put it, we are to rejoice with those who rejoice and weep with those who weep (Romans 12:15). Love unites us in the happiness as well as the sorrow of those we love. Shared joy and shared grief are both signs of true love.

There is, however, a limit to the outer boundary of this sharing. I see on TV, as an example, children bathing and drinking from obviously polluted streams. My heart goes out to them, and I may give a few dollars to help dig water wells to provide fresh, unpolluted water for them. But then I turn to other activities, and these children are forgotten. If, on the other hand, I received word that one of my children is seriously ill, other things would have a much more difficult time capturing my attention. I weep with those who weep more truly when they are close to me.

It turns out that God has created us such that we need love. It is not an option like icing on a cake. It is essential for our humanity. There is a really great country-western song about Little Rock, Arkansas. The singer is in Little Rock, and the woman he loves is somewhere else. He tells her how much he loves and misses her, and the verse ends with the words, "I'm not me without you!"

There is a truth here much deeper than recognized. We both gain and express our identity and our sense of self in interaction with others. And the stronger the connection, the more important that person is to our sense of self. What I have been with Rachel over the years of our marriage is most significant in how I see myself. And how I am with her each day most powerfully expresses that image. That is true because I love her most in the world. I can truly sing that song to her, "I am not me without you."

I recall a cartoon I saw many years ago. The picture was of a strong-looking woman striding toward a closed door. She is dressed in a coat and is carrying a suitcase. She is dragging a man clinging to her leg, and he is pleading, "Don't leave me. I'm deeply in need with you!" Rachel and I frequently refer to this cartoon. It is funny. But it also communicates an important truth. We need to love. God made us that way from conception. We need to love and to receive love. God knew it from the beginning. He said, "It is not good that man should dwell alone." So, he made woman. We find others to love, and we are fulfilled.

Thinking About God Thinking About Me

"If God had a refrigerator, your picture would be on the door."

Author unknown

Psalm 139 may be my favorite psalm. I see David, now an elderly man, sitting at a huge wooden table on one of the many verandas of his Jerusalem palace. It is springtime. The blossoms bloom, the day is bright, and the breezes on his brow are cool. He has ruled a strong and respected nation for forty-one years. Its borders are secure, the nation is robust economically, and its finances are distributed with justice and fairness.

As he reaches for his quill, his hands shake slightly. His muscles are not as strong and quick as they once were. His fingers no longer race across the strings of the harp he has always loved to play. His eyes may have dimmed slightly, but his spirit is strong, and his mind is alert. His heart is filled with love and gratitude as he begins to write. He starts by acknowledging that God knows him. "You have searched me" (Psalm 139:1), he says. Nothing is hidden from God. Perhaps Bathsheba and her husband Uriah and a baby who died are not far from his mind. God knows our thoughts and our words before we speak about them. For David, there is no fear and shame here. God knows all and forgives, protects, and provides. The eye of God is a loving eye.

David continues to write. We can find no place that separates us from the presence of God. He is with us wherever we go. He sees us even in the darkness of night. He knew us while we were still in the womb. Indeed, it was His hand that shaped our being in that hidden place. He knows the days of our life from the beginning, even before they are written in His book. David is overwhelmed, "Such knowledge," he declares, "is too wonderful for me" (Psalm 139:6).

I must admit that I am deeply moved by these words. They are too wonderful for me. Like David, I can look back on many years that confirm the love, protection, and providence of a faithful God. My life, with its share of disappointments, failures, broken hearts, broken promises, sleepless nights, disease, and death, is so wonderful that it stands as ample evidence that affirms that God keeps His word and that David's description of God is true. But David is not finished. He has one more affirmation of God that, frankly, I was not expecting. He announces, "How precious are your thoughts of me!" (Psalm 139:17). Is the eternal, self-sufficient creator God thinking of me? It simply blows my mind that there is room in God for thoughts of one so insignificant and small as I am.

Yet, it is true. I think of the beautiful description of God's love for us that the prophet Zephaniah pictured. He said, "The

Lord your God is with you, he is mighty to save, he will take great delight in you, he will quiet you with his love, he will rejoice over you with singing" (Zephaniah 3:17). My mind draws a picture of a mother at the bedside of her child who is afraid in the dark. She quiets him with love, and she sings over him.

I can remember many nights when our children were small, and one of them would wake in the middle of the night crying. Some of my sweetest memories in those beginning days of fatherhood are of holding that small body in my arms as I sang my child back to sleep. I felt happy, full of love, like a strong parent protective of my little one. Could that be the feelings Zephaniah is describing as God sings over us?

I think of the special words Isaiah uses to picture our relationship with God. He describes God as a mother who has just given birth. We are her newborn baby. "You will nurse and be satisfied at her comforting breasts; you will drink deeply and delight in her overflowing abundance" (Isaiah 66:11).

Adult children can do this for their parents. Let me tell you about Mary Schramski, about whom I wrote in my book *Talking with Ducks*. In November of 1991, she was told that her father was dying. Jim Hauser, a seventy-two-year-old former airline pilot, had an inoperable malignant tumor on his spine. His physicians gave him only a few months to live, at best, and they prescribed radiation treatments and lots of painkilling medicine.

Mary, a community college teacher in Keller, Texas, had spent most of her life separated from her father and did not know him well. She did know that he had never been sick, was careful with his health, and was a long-distance runner. She resolved to spend as much time with him as possible in an effort to get to know this man who was a stranger to her. She resigned from her teaching position and traveled back and forth from her home to Las Cruces, New Mexico, where her father lived. She monitored his heavy daily schedule of painkilling medications and helped him with the radiation treatments.

As predicted by his physicians, his condition worsened. By early January, he refused to eat, would not voluntarily get out of bed, and was deeply depressed. He weighed only 104 pounds and was catharized. He seemed to have lost all hope and was ready to die. In February, Mary resolved to take him home with her. "I wanted my father to die in my home," she explained. Her father's physicians protested that he was too weak to make the trip, but Mary insisted.

Mary resolved to do two things during her father's last days. She would make him as comfortable as possible, and she would do everything she could to get to know as much about him as possible. She spent virtually every minute of the day with him. They talked and shared their lives with each other. She saw to it that he spent some time outside every day. She took him places and devised ways that he could help her with household duties. She altered the medication plan by giving him medications only when he requested them rather than on a rigid hourly schedule.

His requests for medicine came further and further apart, and once, he went three days without any painkillers. He began to feel better, to spend more time out of bed, and was more alert. He could not get enough conversation with Mary and with other members of her family. He began to speak of the future.

Her father did not die. He resumed walking for exercise. He returned to Las Cruces to sell his home there, bought a lot in Keller, and built a home for himself. The last time I spoke to Mary was in 1994. Her father was alive and enjoying life at that time.

How do we explain what happened to this man? No one knows for sure. The radiation treatments may have "cured" his cancer. Or, it may be that Mary's love and his growing love for Mary gave him a reason to live. He had hope and purpose and meaning because he was lovingly connected with someone else. What cured his body, we do not know. But one thing we do know for sure: love turned his life around.

As I listened to Mary's obvious fascination, delight, and unconditional love for her father, I wondered, "Could it be that this is the way that God gazes at each of His children? Does He see me as this woman saw her needy father?" Zephaniah and Isaiah say that He does.

We often say to people things like, "You have been on my mind a lot lately." When someone is about to undergo a difficult experience of some kind or other, we promise, "I'll be thinking about you." We might say when someone is moving away, "I will never forget you." All these are designed to communicate the importance of the other to us. Having someone in our thoughts is a positive expression of high regard, esteem, and love. That is why David could declare, "How precious are your thoughts of me" (Psalm 139:17). And that is why I can say, "You are on His mind a lot lately. He is thinking about you. He will never forget you!"

One Sunday morning years ago, as I made my preparations for church, I heard a man sing a song by Ronald Payne and Ronny Hinson. It brought tears to my eyes. The two verses of the song describe the singer as an ordinary, commonplace human being. No big shakes, nothing special, just an everyday man on the street who makes mistakes and often slips. But the chorus is what the song is about. It declares, *"When he was on the cross, I was on his mind. For he knew me, yet, he loved me. He whose glory makes the heavens shine; so unworthy of such mercy. Yet when he was on the cross, I was on his mind."*[2]

At all times, God is thinking of you. Calvary proves it.

Do You Know the Word "Pusillanimity"?

I didn't. I had seen the word a few times over the years but had never bothered to look it up. I could tell from the context that the word meant something negative, a human trait that one would seek to avoid. Besides, the word looked undesirable. I just knew that one would be insulted if this word was used to describe him. So, I simply read on without taking the time to determine its exact meaning.

And then, a few days ago, there it was on the page facing me. The author said that humility is equally opposed to both "pride and pusillanimity." My curiosity got the best of me. I could see how humility was opposed to pride. Everybody knows that. But pusillanimity? What does that mean, and how is humility opposed to it? I could not go on until I reached for my dictionary.

It turns out that "pusillanimity" means to be "faint-hearted and cowardly." It also means to be "self-deprecating," to "belittle one's self, to express disapproval of one's self." A pusil-

---
[2] Ronald Payne and Ronny Hinson. "When He Was on the Cross." I'm a Jesus Fan. 1984.

lanimous person suffers from an "inferiority complex." Too many Christians fall into that pusillanimous category. They constantly think of themselves as inadequate, as if that greatly pleased God. It is true that mature humility makes us aware of our limitations. But humility, as Jesus demonstrated it, never encourages an attitude of constant self-accusation or disparagement. Cringing inferiority feelings have no place in the Christian faith.

There is a saying that has been making the rounds for the last several years. When asked in greeting, "How you doing?" some people have taken to answering, "Better than I deserve." (I think this comment has been popularized by Dave Ramsey, a man whose economic and money management system I admire and follow.) I cringe at that statement because it simply is not true.

Because we are Christians, we deserve *the best that life has to offer*. Each of us is a "child of the King." God has promised to fill us with peace, to heal our wounds, to set us free from addictions, to rescue us from the grip of modern-day idols, to guide us down paths that lead to meaning and purpose, to empower us to attain the utmost of spiritual growth, to bask in his love, and to meet our needs. Meditate on Psalm 23! You will see what I mean.

I do not wish to be irreverent, but the fact that our father is the king means that each one of us is a prince or a princess! I remember seeing a movie when I was a child made from the book by Mark Twain entitled *The Prince and the Pauper*. It is set in the 1500s in London and is the story of two boys born on the same day who were look-a-likes. Tom was the son of a poverty-stricken, abusive, and alcoholic father. Edward, on the other hand, was the son of the king, Henry VII.

The two boys met and became friends. Through an interesting set of events, Edward (the prince) was mistakenly identified as Tom and thrown out of the palace by the royal guards. The movie was about the strange new life that each lived because of misidentification. Tom, formerly Edward, ended up living with the abusive alcoholic father and suffering all the humiliation associated with poverty, while Edward, who was really Tom, enjoyed all the privileges of royalty.

The truth for a Christian seems to be that we are both these boys. We started as Tom, living in rags, and, through faith, we have been adopted into the family of the king. The king sought us and invited us into his family. He made us his child. The Scriptures describe this event in highly picturesque language. Malachi, as an example, says, "The sun of righteousness will rise with healing in its wings. And you will go out and leap like calves released from the stall" (Malachi 4:2). But we forget our royal place and ignore the privileges and blessings that are rightfully ours. We wander back to the old ways. We live like paupers despite being a prince or a princess.

We easily forget and even take for granted the amazing fact that we can be called God's children. John reminds us of what God did to make that possible. He says, "How great is the love the father has lavished on us, that we should be called children of God!" (1 John 3:1). That we are God's children is based on one fundamental but unimaginable fact: God wants us. Jesus said, "You did not choose me, I chose you" (John 15:16).

God is spirit, is perfect, is eternal, and exists outside both time and space. Humans are physical, imperfect, finite, and are limited by both time and space. How is it possible for a divine spirit to have a relationship of love and communion with beings who are flesh and blood? Philosophers and theologians have pondered that question for centuries. How can such a huge divide be bridged? The distance and the difference between us and God are infinite. It is certainly impossible for us to cross that wide expanse. Yet, the Bible teaches that God can, and He has. He wants us, and He comes for us. He clothed Himself in flesh so as to reveal Himself in terms that we could understand. "To those who receive him, who believe on his name, he gives the right to become children of God" (John 1:12).[3]

The Bible teaches that something really big happens in us when we join the royal family. Something we must never, never forget. Our faith not only makes us a child of the king, but it also places us "in Christ." The words "in Christ," "in the Lord," and "in Him" appear 164 times in the writings of Paul alone. We are told, for example, that we *are created in Him* to *be God's masterpiece* (Ephesians 2:10).

Being in Him changes our life. "If anyone is in Christ, he is a new creature" (2 Corinthians 5:17, NASB). Herein lies the driving force for the entire Christian life, according to Paul. We are "in Christ," and for that reason alone, the old self has died, and God has made all things new. We have become a new creation with a new way of life. Being in Christ, and Christ in us, means that we measure our life according to the standards by which Christ measured His life.

Malcomb Muggeridge, an English author (died 1990), late in his life wrote about how he felt about his accomplishments and

---

[3] Author's translation.

successes in life. He noted that he had achieved a certain level of fame, enjoyed a pleasurable way of life, and had reached a satisfactory level of personal fulfillment. "Multiply these things by a million, add them together, and they are nothing, less than nothing, [...] measured against one drought of that living water that Christ offers to the spiritually thirsty." Always remember and never forget that we drink from that flowing spring of living water because we are a child of the king! No pusillanimity.

The Fifth Sparrow

"Are not five sparrows sold for two pennies? Yet not one of them is forgotten by God. Indeed, the very hairs of your head are numbered. Don't be afraid; you are worth more than many sparrows" (Luke 12:6–7).

Sparrows are the most widely distributed bird in our world. They live comfortably everywhere that people are found on our planet. They are gregarious, social birds living well in association with people. Their plumage, in comparison with other species of birds, is dull and uninteresting. Females are mostly pale brown and grey with specks of white, and males have black and white streaks along with pale brown and grey. They are small, measuring about six inches and weighing only a few ounces.

I suppose that if birds were distributed along some sort of hierarchy, sparrows would be at the bottom. People whose hobby is watching birds (known as "birders") never get excited about seeing a sparrow. Jesus certainly knew that most people in His day saw them as unimportant when He made the comments recorded in Luke 12:5–6.

These verses are a single comment in a list of short statements Jesus is making. The rabbis referred to this kind of teaching as *charaz*, which means "stringing pearls." Jesus' comment about sparrows is one pearl in this string He wants to emphasize. Overall, He is preaching about God's providential care for people and how that care makes our fear unnecessary. Jesus says, "You can purchase five sparrows for two pennies." A penny was the smallest coin at that time and was less than our penny in value. The going price for two sparrows was one penny (Matthew 10:29–31). Buy four for two pennies, and they would throw a fifth sparrow in for free.

That fifth sparrow is the ultimate in worthlessness. He is thrown into the deal as if he has no value at all. He starts out worthless at any price and then is pitched into the mix for free. But here is the zinger: Jesus wants us to know that even this bird, worthless in human eyes, is not forgotten by God. Matthew makes it even more powerful. He says that not even this fifth sparrow dies without God knowing it! This God who marks the death even of a sparrow knows every hair of our head.

Hannah Whitall Smith (1832–1911), a prolific author on Christian subjects, said, "He who counts the very hairs of our head and suffers not a sparrow to fall without him, takes note of the minutest matters that can affect the lives of his children, and regulates them all according to his perfect will, let their origin be what they may." William Shakespeare has one of his characters say, "There is a special providence in the fall of a sparrow,"[4] and still another says, "He that doth the ravens feed, yea, providentially caters for the sparrow."

---
4 Shakespeare, William. Hamlet. In The Complete Works of William Shakespeare. Act 5, Scene 2, Lines 215–217.

No detail escapes the notice of our Father. We can know this for sure about ourselves because it is true even for a fifth sparrow. That is why when we feel insecure about the provisions of life, whatever that may mean to us, Jesus urges us to "consider the birds of the air." We can receive reassurance in how the birds somehow find what they need for life regardless of what the circumstances are.

But I think there is a deeper, more psychological, and equally important consideration in Jesus' comments. I recall that Emily Dickinson, in one of her poems, compares herself to a rich, high-society, aristocratic lady of her day. The woman's breast, she says, "is fit for pearls," and her brow "for thrones." She concludes, "I—a sparrow—build there / sweet with twigs, and twine / My perennial home."[5]

In our own minds, we set up a hierarchy much like the birds. There are the eagles in God's kingdom, along with the ravens, the cute hummingbirds and quail, and the colorful finches and cardinals. In the middle, there are bluebirds, blackbirds, robins, and swallows. Further down the list, there are the blue jays, crows, and cowbirds. And finally, there are sparrows. Too many of God's children cram ourselves into that final category. Like Emily Dickinson, we compare ourselves to the "important" people and think of ourselves as having nothing more to offer than a bird's nest, messy with twigs and string.

The words of Psalm 40:17 (EHV) are true about all of us. David, the king of Israel, admits, "Yet I am poor and needy." None of us can come proudly before God as if He were fortunate to

---

5 Dickinson, Emily. "Her Breast Is Fit For Pearls." The Complete Poems of Emily Dickinson. Edited by Thomas H. Johnson, 1955.

have us on His side. We are limited human beings with a nature that is naturally self-centered and self-interested. We desperately need what God has to offer because He has made us that way. He is the key that unlocks our hearts, and without Him, we are nothing. That much is true for all of us.

But that same David sings, "For you created my inmost being; you knit me together in my mother's womb. I praise you because I am fearfully and wonderfully made" (Psalm 139:13–14). It seems that God reigns over a kingdom of sparrows. But we are each beloved in His sight. He wanted each of us and knew us even before we came to be in our mother's womb. For Him, there is no hierarchy.

I am not very proficient in this area. Throughout my career, I compared myself, as Emily Dickinson did, to those who were more accomplished and seemed to achieve great things for God. One day, I read a comment from Mother Teresa. She was a woman who gave herself in service to the sick and dying in the slums of Calcutta, India (now called Kolkata). The Metropolitan Area has a population of over 15 million, and some call it "the most hopeless city in the world."

Mother Teresa spent her life tending to the physical and spiritual needs of the poorest of the poor, people who had been born, lived, and were now dying in the streets, including children. She brought them into her "hospital," where she and her coworkers tended to their needs until they died. No one ever got well in her hospital. Her mantra was, "They lived like dogs, let them die like persons." Few things in the eyes of our modern world would be less relevant than her life-long work. However, she said, "What you do is not important, but it is very important that you do it."

It is not how many you help that is important. You may work on the level of the sparrow. What is important is that you give yourself fully to the task that is before you. "Brighten the corner where you are" are the words we used to sing in the church where I was growing up. To God, the song of the sparrow is as beautiful and distinctive as that of the bobwhite. Let us all, fifth sparrows, lift our song to Him.

• CHAPTER 2 •

The Path of Faith

In Matthew 11:29 (KJV), Jesus offered the invitation, "Take my yoke upon you and learn of me." Like young oxen, we share with Him the yoke that He wears. And when we do, He teaches us what it means to belong to Him. In essence, He is inviting us to join His school so that we may learn His way of life. Paul said, "We are being transformed into his likeness with ever-increasing glory which comes from the Lord, who is the Spirit" (2 Corinthians 3:18).

On Caterpillars and Butterflies

"Be transformed..." (Romans 12:2).

Is it possible that Christians have lost sight of one of the greatest truths taught in the Bible? Have we forgotten, or did we ever know, Jesus' teaching concerning God's deepest purpose in our lives? The Scriptures teach that God's constant invitations to us derive from His desire to grow us into the person He intended that we be when He created us. For example, Paul says that His constant prayer for the Philippians is that they may be filled with the fruits of righteousness (Philippians 1:9–11). Further, He desires that they may make "progress [...] in the faith" (Philippians 1:25). We know that God wants to "save our souls." Have we forgotten that He wants also to "save our lives"?

There are a number of well-known Bible words that describe that growth and progress. I have in mind words like salvation, conversion, healing, born again, redemption, forgiveness, and sanctification. These words, and others, depict God's desire to be given entry into our lives to make us "new." They describe much more than a single, once-in-a-lifetime experience. They are an ongoing process that extends throughout our life on Earth.

The model that the Scriptures set forth toward which God desires to mold us is none other than Jesus Himself. Ephesians 4:13 says that we will "become mature, attaining to the whole measure of the fullness of Christ." First John 4:17 points out, "As he is, so shall we be in this world." Philippians 1:6 informs us that God has begun a work in us, and He will carry it on until the day of Christ Jesus. The scripture speaks of us becoming a new field in which God sows His seed to produce His crop (1 Corinthians 3:9). Paul clearly states that it is God's purpose that "we are being transformed into his likeness with ever-increasing glory, which comes from the Lord, who is the Spirit" (2 Corinthians 3:18).

Have we come to the place where we give only lip service to the thing which is God's greatest desire for us? Some scholars think so. For example, Roger Scruton, a British contemporary, conservative political philosopher who was a Christian (died 2020), once wrote an essay called "Real Men Have Manners." It was well-written, witty, and thought-provoking, as are all his writings.

In this essay, he notes that Christianity is lived out in social relations. Our faith is never an isolated, private matter. In fact, Jesus said that we are to "go into all the world" to live out our faith so that others will see and "glorify God." Scruton notes that we have a choice in our interactions with other people between "human and merely animal relations." His point is that God's work in us is away from our natural inclination toward animal instincts and toward God's definition of what it means to be human.

As an example, Scruton decries the loss in modern culture of the human quality of "tenderness." He says, "Tender feelings do not exist outside a social context. Tenderness grows out of care and courtesy, out of graceful gestures, out of quiet, attentive concern. It is something you learn, and politeness is a way of practicing it."[6] Animals do not practice tenderness or courtesy. Cows going after hay push others away and "bully" their way to get their own selfish needs met.

Rachel and I have two little dogs, and I often put a little peanut butter on the tip of a finger and let them lick it off. You should see how they push the body of the other away and how they stick their nose in front of the other. Scruton intends to remind us that God's greatest desire is to lift us throughout our lifetime from self-centered animal behavior to loving and tender Christian motivations and behavior.

Paul refers to this deep-seated change that God desires to make in Romans 12:1–2. He says, "Don't conform; be transformed." Don't conform to the world's way of living (animal

---

6 Scruton, R. (2000) Real Men Have Manners, City Journal. Available at: https://www.city-journal.org/article/real-men-have-manners (Accessed: 09 November 2023).

behavior). Conformity has to do with external and malleable standards that change from day to day and follow popular philosophy and the newest fad. Paul is saying, "Don't use these standards to measure your progress in life."

Rather, Paul counsels, "Be transformed." Unlike conformity, which has to do with external things, transformation has to do with the core of our being, our identity. It is our anchor. It is that which we possess permanently. We get our word *metamorphosis* from the Greek word Paul uses here. Notice that he does not say, "Transform yourself." This deep inner change is done as a gift from God. It is not something that we can do for ourselves. When it is done right, it is like a caterpillar spinning a cocoon around itself and being transformed into a butterfly. It loses the essence of a caterpillar and becomes the essence of a butterfly. It no longer crawls. Now, it flits and flies from flower to flower. It started as one thing and became something entirely different. That is what God desires to do for us. We start as a caterpillar, and God makes us into a butterfly.

Victoria Erickson, creative writer and writing coach, reminds us that transformation is a grueling process. She writes, "Transformation is not sweet and bright, it's a dark and murky, painful pushing. An unraveling of the untruths we have carried in our body. A practice of facing our own created demons. A complete uprooting before becoming." Did you know that many caterpillars refuse to enter a cocoon? They live their entire life as a caterpillar and never fulfill their destiny to become a butterfly. When we enter that cocoon, we face the unknown. There is a time in the cocoon when the life that is there is neither a caterpillar nor a butterfly. For the caterpillar, the cocoon is like death.

Many Christians are like that unwilling caterpillar. We are satisfied being whatever we are. We do not want the work, the heavy responsibility, or the uncertainty of change. We refuse growth and cling to the familiar. We are not good at recognizing our illusions about ourselves. We overlook our weaknesses and become experts at justifying our self-proclaimed reality. We say things like, "I'm a good person." Or, "God loves me just like I am." (Both of which are true but can never be used as an excuse!)

The secret of transformation and spiritual growth is "submission." That is also what makes growth very hard. We give ourselves to the Lord. We submit to Him. We open our heart's door and invite Him to come in and be the center of our life. That is not easy for a human being to do. But one thing I know for sure. No butterfly ever regrets the day he entered the cocoon!

When Climbing, Take Little Steps

He wanted Everest in a day: if it took two, he lost interest.
John Fowles

Friedrich von Hugel (died in 1925) was an Austrian nobleman and Christian apologist. He knew a thing or two about hiking the majestic mountains of his country and sometimes likened the Christian life to ascending those rugged but beautiful trails. Experienced mountaineers, he once wrote, "have a quiet, regular, short step" which they can "keep up, on and on as they ascend." In contrast, "the inexperienced townsman hurries along, and soon has to stop, dead beat with the climb." If you wish to grow in faith and serve God and love Christ, you must "make them a slow and sure and utterly real" upward climb.

Reading Hugel's advice took me back to my younger adult days when I was a runner. I loved races and spent many Saturdays at special runs of seven or ten miles. I could tell within the first quarter mile those persons whom I would soon pass as they walked exhaustedly along. They were the ones who burst from the starting line to take a fast-paced lead. Better, I knew, to be like the slow-footed but steady tortoise in Aesop's Fables who beat the fleet but overconfident hare in a race.

Jeremiah, I think, would be comfortable with these ideas. In fact, he described his ministry among the Jews in words that fit these very concepts. It was the "fourth year of Jehoiakim, king of Judah," which would be 605 BC, and the army of Nebuchadnezzar, the new king of Babylon, was marching even now toward the gates of Jerusalem. They were fresh from the defeat of the army of Egypt and had lowered their sights on Judah. There was no way that the feeble army of Jehoiakim could withstand the coming onslaught. A dark night was lowering itself upon the people of God.

Jeremiah declared, "For twenty-three years, … the word of the Lord has come to me and I have spoken to you again and again, but you did not listen" (Jeremiah 25:3). Jeremiah is certainly describing his job as an uphill climb. It is not easy to face for years a task that is met with rejection and defiance. Even tougher, the people to whom he spoke were his kinsmen whom he loved. He took no pleasure in the message he delivered. Yet he has continued in his calling. He has spoken the words of God to his countrymen "again and again."

The Hebrew word translated as "again and again" is *hashkem* (ha-sh-keem). It is an interesting word with an unusual history. It comes from the Hebrew word that means "shoulder" and came to be associated with placing your pack on your shoulder and setting off for a long journey. The noun becomes a verb that means "carrying a burden patiently for a long time." It means "to persist," to be obstinately and tenaciously stubborn in some activity, and to hold firmly and steadfastly to some purpose despite obstacles and setbacks. It means to keep going and never quit.

The word *hashkem* is at the center of Jeremiah's life as well as his book. It is found twelve times in his writings, beginning in chapter 7 and continuing until chapter 44. Eugene Peterson says, "We know that Jeremiah suffered an enormous amount of abuse across his years. He faced mockery and rejection and imprisonment. He wrestled with stretches of discouragement and pits of despair and thoughts of quitting. What difference does it make anyway?"[7] Yet, for twenty-three years, he rose each morning before sunrise and opened his ears to hear the word of the Lord. Each day, he went into the streets faithfully to announce that word to the people. No one listened. Yet he persisted. For twenty-three years, he persisted.

God once asked him, "If you get tired running a footrace, how will you do against horses?" (Jeremiah 12:5). I think Jeremiah did pretty well against horses. Six hundred-five BC was exactly 2628 years ago. People down through the centuries

---

[7] Eugene Peterson, Run with the Horses, (Illinois: Intervarsity Press, 2009), p.109.

have listened to Jeremiah's message and been moved by it. The "weeping prophet," as he was known, has impacted millions across the years. He has stirred untold numbers to stand in the face of tough sledding.

Even Jesus was encouraged by Jeremiah's powerful witness. He quoted directly from Jeremiah on at least two occasions. Jesus had in mind the book of Lamentations, written by Jeremiah, as He wept over Jerusalem (Matthew 23:37–39). The same spirit that moved Jeremiah moved Jesus as He contemplated the destruction of the city of God. And when He overthrew the money changers' tables in the temple and ran the unethical sellers of sacrificial animals from the temple (Luke 19:45–48), He quoted Jeremiah 7:11, "Has my house which bears my name become a den of robbers?"

Don't feel sorry for Jeremiah. He was not stuck with a dirty job that he could not avoid. He was committed to a purpose, and, as such, he is an example to the rest of us. We need a bunch of *hashkem* today.

The Bible is full of exhortations to persistence. Proverbs 24:16 says, "The righteous person falls seven times and each time rises again." That piece of wisdom reminds me of the comment by Winston Churchill, "Success is stumbling from failure to failure with no loss of enthusiasm."

Galatians 6:9 encourages, "Do not grow weary with doing good." Hebrews 12:1 reminds us to "run with endurance the race set before you." I especially like the admonition to Christian men found in 1 Corinthians 16:13–14, "Be on your guard; stand firm in the faith; be men of courage; be strong. Do everything in love."

Jesus once told a story designed to encourage His disciples to pray and not give up (Luke 18:1–8). It is a story of a widow and an indifferent judge. This widow petitioned the judge with a grievance, only asking that she be treated with justice. She sought no special favors. She was asking only for fairness. The judge spurned her request time and again. But she persisted and refused to give up. She kept at him until he relented. "I don't care about God or man. Yet because this widow keeps bothering me, I will see that she gets justice before she wears me out" (Luke 18:5). Jesus praised the widow for her *hashkem*.

Hashkem gets us up before daybreak. Not everyone is an early riser, but I am. I never get over the coming of dawn. Everything is new. It is a new start, a new beginning, a resurrection. I get to live a new day for the Lord. I ask for strength. I ask for *hashkem*. And God delivers, and I take small steps upward.

What Ever Happened to Sin?

"For all have sinned and fall short of the glory of God" (Romans 3:23).

We don't hear the word "sin" much anymore. Certainly, it is not used often, if at all, in everyday conversation. Who wants to mention "downers" in a talk designed to pass the time pleasantly? You might hear the word once in a while in political or entertainment circles. But those references serve most often a facetious, non-serious purpose. We might hear Las Vegas called "Sin City," or some pundit may refer to a "night of sin" or "sinful woman." These terms are accompanied by a wink and a nod. The mayor of New Orleans once welcomed a meeting of a philosophical society by telling them that in New Orleans, there is "much sin but little crime."

Sin, even in church, appears to be a dead word. We churchgoers are much more comfortable with euphemisms like "mistakes," "blunders," and even "moral problems." The demise of sin at church began with the publication of Joseph Fletcher's *Situation Ethics* in 1952. Fletcher, an ordained Methodist minister, not only wrote about "ethical offenses" but considered them created by a warped society that no longer teaches us how to love. People caught up in these "miscalculations" and "misunderstandings" are not personally responsible for their "misdeeds," and their unfortunate situation can be remedied by simply teaching them how to be smarter and stronger and do the loving thing.

Sin is considered to be a harsh word, a hangover of an earlier time when religion was less sophisticated or relevant. Its usage today is limited to those contexts in which one seeks a half-jovial, mildly facetious word. But in letting the word sin die, have we not lost something very real and very necessary in this hard-driving and secular world? In debunking this old-fashioned word, haven't we lost a piece of ourselves, a necessary piece for living a fulfilling life?

T. S. Eliot, a critically acclaimed poet and playwright who became a Christian in his adult years, has brilliantly shown in his play *The Cocktail Party* how modern persons carry beneath the surface a recognition of the reality of sin. In one skillful scene, he shows how necessary that recognition is to human beings. The story deals with a young woman named Celia who suddenly has a flashing insight into a significant part of her life. She has for some time carried on an amorous affair with a married man, a relationship which she had previously found satisfying. She suddenly realizes that she has been selfish and vain from the beginning of this relationship, and this unsought insight shakes her to the deepest place of her heart.

Having no place else to turn, Celia speaks with her physician about her experience. Celia recognizes that "something is wrong with me. The only word I can find for it is a sense of sin." She explains that she had been brought up to disbelieve in sin or to consider it "bad form or psychological." Yet, she admits, "this may be more real than anything I believed in." It is a "feeling of emptiness, of failure toward something, or someone, outside myself. I feel I must *atone*."[8]

What is important for me in this story is that the feelings and thoughts that Celia confronts lie buried beneath the conscious minds of *all* people. Celia let them come out, but the majority of us keep them hidden, covered over with rationalizations, excuses, and material objects that capture our attention, with fantasies of our well-being, with comparisons with other "average" people whom we see as happy and successful. We develop defense mechanisms to keep these truths from coming into our conscious awareness. I honestly believe that these inner struggles are the source of most of our stress, anxiety, fear, and so-called mental disorders.

What I am saying is that we need the concept of sin to help us maintain a sense of stability and to make sense of life. For example, there must be certain boundaries beyond which one may not stray and certain acts one must execute satisfactorily

---

8 Eliot, T.S. *The Cocktail Party*. New York. 1948.

and according to rules if any game is to be enjoyed. From kid's play, like jump rope and hide-and-seek, all the way to adult games of cards and professional sports, rules give the behavior a sense of meaning and purpose. They help shape preparation for the event, and they give both participants and spectators a sense of anticipation.

What is true in games of play is equally true in morals. The word sin in the New Testament is a translation of the Greek word *hamartia* (ha-mar-te-ah). It was actually used in the world of games before it came to have a religious sense. It means simply "to miss the mark." In archery, one aims at a bullseye and lets the arrow fly. It hits, or it misses the mark. If it misses, one is filled, like Celia, with a sense of loss, emptiness, and even guilt. To sin, i.e., to "miss the mark," reminds us that the mark is significant!

The destructiveness of sin and its negative consequences is far more serious than missing a shot in the game of basketball. Martin Buber, a Jewish philosopher of great repute, says that we should translate the word for sin in the Old Testament as "highwayman." For him, sin lurks behind castle gates to take our possessions and our lives. This certainly is a New Testament idea. One may be "dead in sin" (Ephesians 2:1), "in bondage of sin" (Romans 6:23), "corrupted by sin" (Colossians 2:13), or "separated from God by sin" (1 Timothy 5:6). To miss the mark morally is no small, laughing matter.

The bullet that took the life of Martin Luther King Jr. on April 4, 1968, did not miss its mark. But the finger of James Earl Ray, which pulled the trigger of the rifle, most assuredly did. We can only guess what was in his heart that day that enabled him to kill a fellow human being. The implements used by a skilled physician who takes the life of an unborn baby do not miss their mark. Again, we cannot know what is in the heart of that person who has vowed to save life and yet ends the life of a fellow human being. We may conclude as Josef Pieper, quoting Thomas Aquinas, said, "When we consider both men as moral persons, [...] 'their failings are glaring.'" The mark they missed is the most glaring.

We have lost much when we surrendered this powerful word. It teaches humility because we do not get to determine the end or the goal. Direction in life is not left to arbitrary choice. The standards are outside ourselves. That simple fact provides direction to meaning and purpose. The game makes sense. Morality calls us to involve the whole of the human self. No piece of life is left untouched, and we are steered to a life of fulfillment. Having a standard outside ourselves makes us responsible and accountable for the freedom to decide. The game gets exciting!

The recognition of our sins opens the door for faith. To return for a moment to Celia of T.S. Eliot's play, her sense of sin made her uncomfortable, which aroused in her the need for atonement.

Faith Conquers Fear

"Do not be anxious about anything, but in everything, by prayer and petition, with thanksgiving, present your requests to God. And the peace of God, which transcends all understanding, will guard your hearts and minds in Christ Jesus" (Philippians 4:6–7).

In his 1933 inaugural address, Franklin Delano Roosevelt famously said, "All we have to fear is fear itself."[9] That was a tall order back then, and it remains so today. It seems that fear is a rational response to the ominous circumstances we face in our world. Powerful men and women whom we don't even know hold in their hands the ability to make decisions that impact our lives in awesome ways. All around us, civilization seems to be crumbling. Institutions like the family, church, communities, and schools that once held society together stand on wobbly legs.

Biologists Heather Heying and Bret Weinstein, authors of *A Hunter-Gather's Guide to the 21st Century*, present a strong case that we have created a civilization for which we are biologically and psychologically inadequate. We remain hunter-gatherers living in the crowded, impersonal, noisy "concrete jungle." It turns out that there is much that causes us to fear. Each of us could make a detailed list of the many threats we face in today's troubled world. And we are rightfully concerned about these threats to our children and grandchildren.

To top it off, there is deeper fear, a fear that stems from no particular, observable threat. It is called anxiety, and it is more like a free-floating state of chronic, generalized apprehensiveness that stems from no particular, observable threat. One may feel a sense of nervous uneasiness in reaction to stress, perceived danger, or even an unfamiliar situation. It may result in muscular tension, sleep disorders, perspiration, elevated blood pressure, increased heart rate, or heart palpitations. One often responds to this painful condition with an inordinate need to

---

9 Franklin Roosevelt, 1932. FDR Inaugural Speech.

control everything. For most, anxiety merely takes the fun out of living. For others, it can become completely debilitating.

I've read that the Bible says, "Do not be afraid" 365 times. Once for each day of the year. I have not counted them, nor do I know a reliable source that confirms this number. But I do know that Jesus frequently spoke about fear and worry. The teaching of the Scripture is that Christians have no need for worry, and that is why Jesus can say, "Do not be anxious." This statement opens up two questions: First, can we take such a statement seriously? And second, in this troubled world, how can we not be anxious? The answer to the first question is "yes." Let me tell you a story to answer the second.

We may call this tale a "short story" because it has only three lines. Despite its brevity, it has all the qualities which characterize excellent fiction. It has a bad guy who comes only to destroy. It has a good guy who comes heroically to save. And it has a time of suspense as to the outcome and a happy conclusion. All this in three lines, and, even more importantly, the story tells us how to completely defeat anxiety. Here it is:

Fear knocked at my door.
Faith answered the knock.
No one was there!

I wish to be simple and direct without being simplistic. Faith is a power in our hands (or heads) that is like dynamite. It is explosive and rearranges things in unexpected and startling ways. Paul says, "You are saved by grace through faith" (Ephesians 2:8, CSB). Faith does not save. God's grace (His favor, unconditional love, forgiveness freely given) saves, but faith is the avenue by which grace travels to us! Get that. Understand it.

Our faith opens the door to God's awesome *power*. Our faith accepts God's invitation to heal us, make us new, and rearrange the mess we make of our lives. It is true that faith opens heaven's door to let us in. But also, and this is our point here, faith opens the door of our heart to let God in with His dynamite now before we get to heaven's gate.

This faith is more than accepting a few facts about God. It is much more radical than that. It begins with a clear-eyed understanding that we ourselves are unable to direct our lives. On our own, we are like a turtle I met one day years ago on my walk through the woods. He had somehow got himself upside down in a horse's track made when the trail was muddy. The ridges that the horse's hoof had made in the soft mud had hardened in the hot, dry weather. To make it worse for the turtle, a root from an oak tree lined one side of the bowl in which he was upside-down.

I could see the scuff marks his head had made in the dirt, so I knew he had tried to push himself right-side-up for some time. But the ridges were too much for him. He was struck and would surely die without help. I reached down and set him free. I wish that I could tell you that he stopped long enough to thank me. But, alas, he scuttled for the tallgrass at the trail's edge without so much as a "how-do-you-do!" When we are "on our own," trying to make it without God, we are the "stuck-in-the-dirt" turtle.

Our Christian faith is the pathway God travels to get to us. But it is more. Our faith is a radical entrusting of our life, our being, to God. One writer calls it "abandoning ourselves to the will of God." It is trust in its most radical form. Faith places us like clay in the potter's hand, or a piece of stone yielded to the sculpture's chisel, or the keys of the piano awaiting the fingers of the pianist. Faith says, "Here is my life; make of it what you wish." Nothing less than this deserves to be called "faith."

I'll give you an example from the horse world. Over the years, I have taught many horses to walk willingly across a blue plastic tarpaulin. (In horse shows, such a tarp is used to simulate a water obstacle.) It is one of the toughest exercises for a horse. That is because a horse is colorblind, and the tarp looks to him like a bottomless black hole in the ground. The first time he approaches it, he refuses to go near it. He lowers his head, snorts at it, and backs quickly away. He turns sideways and walks around it. Over time (days or even weeks), he finally puts a foot on it, and one day he willingly walks across it.

Are you able to see the immense trust in his rider that a horse must have to step out into a bottomless black hole in the ground? It makes no sense to him; he can see no logical reason to do such a thing. But it makes sense to the rider. He knows the plan, and he knows that his plan does nothing but good for the horse. To put a horse through this exercise demands trust on the part of the horse, and, interestingly, it also develops greater trust and deepens the relationship between horse and rider. This deeper relationship between the horse and rider, based on trust and respect, is the goal of all proper horse training. And that deeper relationship is what God seeks in all the "exercises" He puts us through in our training.

Can you see how this kind of faith takes the teeth out of worry and anxiety? I can trust this God in Whom I believe because

I know that everything, yes everything without exception that God does, produces good in my life. Nothing is random, and nothing is lost, and nothing is senseless. It all fits into God's plan. That is why the Bible can say simply, "Be anxious for nothing" (Philippians 4:6, NASB).

There is an interesting word in German that deals with the question of faith in God. It is *Kohlerglaube*, which means "charcoal burner's faith." It goes back to the story of a "charcoal burner" (a poor man who used charcoal to heat his house and cook his food). Such a man was once met on a bridge in Prague, the story goes, by a learned scholar who asked, "What do you believe?" He answered, "I believe what the Bible believes." To some, this may seem a nonsensical answer from an ignorant mind. To me, his reply was intelligent, to the point, and perfectly acceptable. While I do not yet know everything that the Bible teaches, like this common man in Germany, I believe it all.

But I do not consider this to be "blind faith," not at all. There is strong and reasonable evidence upon which I base my faith in the God of the Bible. These things are "evidence," not "proof." (If we have proof, we no longer need faith.) But they are, for me, strong and convincing evidence. The purpose of the Bible is to reveal God. From the first to the last page, the stories told and the historical events carefully described are there to reveal God.

The universe convinces any but the most closed mind that there is an intelligent, creative, innovative, imaginative, and inventive force that brought all this into being. The Bible painstakingly describes the nature and character of this supernatural power. I do not claim too much when I say that I admire and want to know better the God therein described. I like this God better than those gods described in any other book or philosophy. I find the way of life that the God of the Bible advocates to be superior to any other lifestyle described in any other religion or philosophy. I want the God of the Bible to be the God of the universe.

It is true that Richard Dawkins, a British biologist and world-famous atheist, has said that the most wicked and undesirable being in all the world is the Old Testament God. Dawkins has revealed his own ignorance of both the Old Testament and the God described therein. Let him read Isaiah and Hosea and think carefully about the God described in these two books alone.

We believers know that the God revealed in Jesus is exactly the God revealed in the Old Testament. It is that God that I want to know because when faith in that God answers the knock at my door, there is no one there!

An Ant of Extraordinary Valor

"I have seen the stars,[...] In my own darkness."
Federico Garcia Lorca

Federico Garcia Lorca is considered one of the greatest Spanish poets of the twentieth century (died in 1936). His poem entitled "The Encounters of an Adventurous Snail" is the story of a serene yet adventurous, gentle creature of the woodland who travels about the forest, seeing what he can see. He meets up with other individuals who catch his attention. He stops for conversation, and then, his curiosity satisfied, he moves on.

Among all the experiences of the inquisitive snail, by far, the most interesting for me is his meeting with a group of ants. One ant, not careful where he was walking, bumped into a tree trunk and decided to climb up the tree. It was the tallest in the forest, and he climbed to the tip-top. What a view! For the first time, he saw the stars, like eyes peering back at him from the darkness. He had never in his life been so moved, touched by the reality and mystery of the heavens.

Returning to the earth, to his natural environment, the inspired ant could not restrain himself from sharing his experience. He went about exclaiming, "There are stars. You can see them if you would look up." To the surprise of the snail, his fellow ants pounced on him, hitting him and pummeling him with sticks, intent on silencing his foolish talk. He had broken the ant code, which declared that the purpose of all ants is to work. They are to stay busy accomplishing things. They don't waste time looking up to see useless things like "stars," whatever stars are.

This portion of Lorca's poem brought to my mind the experience of Jesus. He went about telling people that there are wonderful things in what He called a "spiritual world." There is a reality that is above our natural world of material things, a reality that we can access in our darkness. We can "see" this reality and realize that it is "seeing" us. Jesus is telling us that there is a world far above the material world in which we live. It is a world of beauty, joy, love, and grace. We can access it if only we would look up. It is a world of stars in our darkness that we can look at and come to realize that they are looking back at us.

Many of the stories Jesus told illustrate this truth. Think, for example, of the Good Samaritan. He was making his way down the steep and isolated roadway from Jerusalem to Jericho. He was in enemy territory, being a Samaritan in the land of the Jews. Beyond that danger, this road was infamous for the brigands that hid away in its remoteness to attack unsuspecting travelers.

As he made his way, he came upon a Jewish man who had been set upon by thieves who beat him and robbed him, leaving him to die. Others had seen the wounded traveler and passed him by. The Samaritan, however, stopped and rendered aid, cleaning the man's wounds and transporting him on his own donkey to an inn. There, he paid for the man's care and promised when he made his return trip, he would pay any additional expense the innkeeper had incurred.

Jesus used this story to answer a lawyer's question, "Who is my neighbor?" Of course, Jesus' story answers that question clearly and unambiguously. My neighbor is anyone who needs my help. But it answers many other questions, also. One of the most important of those questions is, "Why should I offer help to anyone?" The story tells us something about the reality of that unseen world Jesus came to tell us about. There is something unique about human beings that goes beyond the material world and impels us to render aid to someone who is hurting. We are more than animals that have accidentally come to exist through purposeless and blind forces. We are not just a piece of flesh. We are a soul that God Himself desired and individually created in His own image (see Psalm 139 and Jeremiah 1:4–5).

Further, the wounded Jew lying in the ditch by the side of the road needed something from the Samaritan. But it is equally true that the Samaritan needed something from the wounded man. We cannot forget that the wounded man needed help, *and the helping man needed to help.* The Jew gave the Samaritan something that the Samaritan greatly needed. He gave him the opportunity to grow to be more like God, the loving creator. Any connection that we establish with another person energizes the potential within us to create and enjoy a deeper relationship with God, with others, and with ourselves. This is why Jesus told us to love even our enemies. Giving away love makes us a more loving person and more capable of receiving love!

In one of his poems, the British poet John Keats referred to the world as "the vale of soul-making." Keats describes life as a valley where "the heart must feel and suffer in a thousand diverse ways." Going to the trouble and expense of helping others, and especially an enemy, feeling what they feel and offering a hand of encouragement and assistance, in Keats' view, is "soul-making." Never forget that following Jesus and living our life with Him as our model builds our souls. Helping others helps us as much, if not more, than the one we help. Those who refused to offer aid to the wounded man by passing by on the other side missed this opportunity for inner growth.

I think it is interesting that Lorca's poem tells us that the little ant "bumped into the trunk of the tree" as if by accident. Isn't this the way life generally works? Those experiences that help us see the stars and change our lives in radical ways often happen to us as if by accident. Someone has said life is what happens to us when we are going somewhere else. Think of your spouse and other significant people in your life. Where were you going when you "bumped" into them? What about life-changing ideas that you have had along the way that just seemed to jump out of nowhere into your thinking?

Last of all, our brave little ant, who had the courage to climb and see the stars and could not restrain speaking of that other world, paid dearly for his experience. So did Jesus, and so will we. Jesus said that the material world resented Him, and it will resent us. To my thinking, it is worth it. I refuse to limit my life to scurrying about the fallen leaves and dirt of the material world just to find my next meal. I have seen the stars! And I refuse to be silent.

Mustard Seed Faith

"We hope your faith will grow" (2 Corinthians 10:15, NLT).

At first glance, it appears that Jesus did not put much stock in the size of faith. Several times, He referred approvingly to "faith the size of a mustard seed." Invariably, He noted the amazing results that such a tiny faith could accomplish. He said that the tiny mustard seed was the smallest of all seeds known in His day and that with a faith that size, one could cast a tree into the ocean or move a mountain from one place to another (Luke 17–6; Matthew 13:32–33). On one occasion, His praise of faith the size of a mustard seed even came in response to His disciples' request, "Increase our faith" (Luke 17:5).

Yet, on several occasions, Jesus seemed to be annoyed with the size of the disciples' faith. He called them "ones of little faith" (see, for example, Matthew 16:8). On many occasions, He emphasized the struggle and turmoil, even persecution, that putting faith in Him would bring into a person's life. He seemed at that point to be encouraging solid, persevering, strong faith to get believers through the hard days that were to come (Matthew 5:11–12). Many of His parables were stories that praised people of great risk, demanded great faith, and censured people who were fearful and had little faith (for example, Matthew 25:14–30). He once described a woman as having "great faith" (Matthew 15:28).

Further, the rest of the New Testament is replete with calls for growth in faith. For example, Paul tells the Corinthians that he hopes his influence would help them grow in faith (2 Corinthians 10:15). He looks forward to visiting the church at Thessalonica to "strengthen you in your faith" (1 Thessalonians 3:2). In 2 Thessalonians, he commends the church because "your faith is growing" (2 Thessalonians 1:3). Peter and the writer of Hebrews admonish their readers not to be satisfied to remain as immature children and babies in the faith but to strive to grow toward adulthood (1 Peter 2:2; Hebrews 6:1).

Was Jesus suggesting by His words about mustard seed faith that we may be satisfied with the tiny faith we have when we become Christians? And, if not, what then did He have in mind? Without a doubt, Jesus, during His growing up years in Nazareth, had worked with His parents in the small family garden. He knew firsthand the power of a seed. By being put on the warm, moist earth, a seed comes alive and initiates a process that naturally fulfills the potential of the seed. Mustard seeds, despite being tiny, contain an inner power that matures to a tree in which birds may nest. Seeds produce if properly tended. They create and sustain life.

Jesus' intent is not to praise the size of faith but to underscore its productive power. Life lies at the heart of faith just as it does at the heart of a seed. Like a seed, faith reminds us that there are things that are unseen that are as real as things we see. It tells us that there are things we do not understand but to which we have access. Faith is not a list of facts that we mentally accept as true. It is a thousand times more powerful than that. It is like a seed that falls among weeds and on hard ground, as in Jesus' parable of the Sower (Luke 8:1–8).

We live in a world of dragons breathing fire that seek to destroy us. The enemy seeks to make us doubt, to give in to our appetites, to waste our talents with cheap games, to fill our minds with trash, to seek ways to cheat others, to hold our gifts with a tight fist, to put ourselves and our pleasure ahead of everything else. He seeks to destroy the seed so that its life-giving power never sees the light of day.

Mustard seed faith can defeat the dragons. Jesus clearly had the power of the seed in mind when He told His disciples, "I tell you the truth, unless a grain of wheat falls into the ground and dies, it remains only a single seed" (John 12:24). Again, He remembers His experience in the family garden. A seed's life-generating power remains unexpressed until it is thrown into the darkness of the earth. There, the seed surrenders itself in the act of fulfilling its natural potential.

This truth is a law of life. Mustard seed faith calls us to trust Him so completely that we put ourselves in situations where all will be lost if He does not come through. The seed of faith grows only in those places where faith is a must. We find ourselves in a place where all we have left is faith. Our ability to control a situation or to control the people around us is at an end. All we have left is the promises of God. When we are at the end of our rope, all that is left is our faith. But mustard seed faith is mighty when we are out of rope.

Harold Kushner is an American rabbi whose son died at age fourteen from progeria (premature aging disease). Writing about that experience, he said,

> People who pray for miracles usually don't get miracles. But people who pray for courage, for strength to bear the unbearable, for the grace to remember what they have left behind instead of what they have lost, very often find their prayers answered. Their prayers help them tap hidden reserves of faith and courage that were not available to them before.

Mustard seed faith expands when dropped into the darkness of the unknown. That faith is like the roots of a mature tree, which clings harder when countering strong winds. The seed opens to new life, and that life is what spiritual growth is all about. Paul had that in mind when he wrote, "I have been crucified with Christ (like the dying seed), and I no longer live but Christ lives in me (the new plant). The life I live in the body, I live by faith in the Son of God" (Galatians 2:20).[10]

It is not the size of one's faith that counts. What matters in the final analysis is the size of the God toward whom the faith is directed. Faith says that what God has promised in the Bible will come to pass. The believer trusts in that God. He or she surrenders to that God. He or she bases their life on that God.

King David ends Psalm 92 with a sweeping declaration that lifts our hearts to sing about the new life faith can give us. He

---
10 Words within parenthesis added by the author.

says, "The godly will flourish like palm trees and grow strong like the cedars of Lebanon. Even in old age they will produce fruit; they will remain vital and green. They will declare that the Lord is good! He is my rock!" (Psalm 92:12; 14–15, NLT). The tiny mustard seed faith can become the mighty oak. I want that, don't you?

• CHAPTER 3 •

The Path of Hope

Tom Bodett, author and radio personality, once said, "They say that a person needs only three things to be happy in this world: someone to love, something to do, and something to hope for."[11] I think that Jesus would agree with Bodett's view. Further, He offers all three things to those who accept His invitation to follow Him.

Our God Is Marching On

"Mine eyes have seen the glory of the coming of the Lord; …. His truth is marching on."

Julia Ward Howe (1861)[12]

Our God is never surprised by the whims of history. He is never outfoxed by the rationality, or lack of it, of human beings. Disease and wars and droughts and stock market surges (up or down) and new technological advances or even the unpredictable quirks of the young do not shock Him or catch Him unprepared.

---
11 A quote by Tom Bodett (no date) Goodreads. Available at: https://www.goodreads.com/quotes/132967-they-say-a-person-needs-just-three-things-to-be (Accessed: 10 November 2023).
12 Julia Ward Howe, "The Battle Hymn of the Republic." 1861.

We who are committed to Him may be astonished or even feel defeated by sudden, unexpected changes, and we may not see the hand of God at work. We may wonder where He is and what He is up to. But, for sure, He has not retreated in defeat, nor has He removed His powerful hand from the rudder to allow the ship to drift any which way. We may be unprepared, but not God. We may not know where He is, but He constantly knows where we are. Listen to the words of Psalm 139:7–12:

> Where can I go from your spirit? Where can I flee from your presence? If I go up to the heavens, you are there; if I make my bed in the depths, you are there. If I rise on the wings of the dawn, if I settle on the far side of the sea, even there your hand will guide me, your right hand will hold me fast. If I say, "Surely the darkness will hide me and the night become light around me," even the darkness will not be dark to you; the night will shine as the day, for the darkness is light to you.

Looking back in history, including biblical history, we observe a surprising fact: *God most frequently shows up in tumultuous times.* That fact is evident in the second verse of the Bible. The earth was formless and empty, and darkness covered the restless and surging waters. And the Spirit of God hovered over those agitated waters (Genesis 1:2) and transformed the chaos into order, beauty, and light. In the first few seconds of time, His mighty hand began to bring life and goodness where formerly there was nothing.

The flood was another time when the earth was tormented by chaos and disorganization. God found a way to begin anew with a weak human being and his family. Or, how about the Exodus? All was turmoil for the people of God. They struggled under the heel of the king of Egypt as slaves, making bricks for his monuments. God was there and, again, using a man of weakness, found a way to bring His people out to freedom.

I could go on in Old Testament stories that demonstrate God's habit of making His hand known and using history to achieve His plan, especially in troubled times. But let me skip to the New Testament and consider the apex of God's mysterious practice of speaking most eloquently in the midst of humanity's most troubling and destructive tendency.

History's most stupendous and necessary act occurred in Jerusalem about 30 AD. God allowed Himself to be killed in humanity's desire to rid itself forever of God. Hebrews 1:3 tells us Jesus is "the radiant light of God's glory and the perfect copy of his nature." John 1:1 identifies Jesus as the Word who was with God and was God.

The supremely impressive, complex, and entirely unexpected figure of Jesus of Nazareth is the central person in this story of God's unpredictability. God, the infinite Creator of the universe, became a baby in Bethlehem's manger and died as a tortured criminal at the hands of corrupt religious and governmental officials. Out of that day, the darkest and most horrid of all human history arose the greatest and most profound revelation of who God is and His unconditional love for us. Only a divine mind working in the shadows of the unknown could have devised such a tale.

Western history is likewise filled with such examples of God showing up in the darkest days. For example, consider the growth of the church beginning with only 120 initial persons, bringing the greatest military power in ancient history (the Roman Empire) to its knees. The development of monasteries in medieval times (called the Dark Ages) to preserve the Bible in written form. The Reformation was another. Finally, there were the wars and bloodshed that were necessary to translate the Bible from Latin into English.

That brings us to today. Modern secularism, with its attendant atheism, began with the movement called the "Enlightenment" in the 1700s. The philosophy that dominated (and still dominates) this movement is based on four tenets:

1. Human rationality is sufficient to solve all problems,
2. Humans, by nature, are good. Unreasonable social rules about morals are what ruin people. (Socialism emerges from this concept.)
3. The flow of history is moving in a positive and upward direction, which nothing can interrupt. Progress is inevitable.
4. God is a fictional ploy made up by the powerful in order to keep the weak in line.

This godless philosophy has served as the foundation for untold instances of human misery. In the twentieth century alone, over fifty million persons were killed in the war. Indeed, this was the bloodiest century in history. In the US, since 1973, over sixty million babies have been aborted as a result of this ideology. Despite its obvious limitations and destructive human results, this philosophy remains the ruling creed of the culture in which we live. It is more powerful than we know, and it dominates the media, the academy, and the political elite. But, and this is the point of this essay, something is moving in our culture! And therein lies our hope.

Once, there was a man who had to travel at night from his home village to a neighboring village to fetch a doctor for his sick wife. It was a moonlit night, but clouds often covered the moon and put him in total darkness. He was not at all sure of the path to his destination, but he trudged on. Suddenly, he was aware that something was out there in the darkness. At first, he was slightly alarmed. And he noticed that if he moved faster, the thing moved faster. If he slowed, the thing slowed. He became terrified.

But he kept going, and it seemed that luck was with him. When, for example, he came to a river, it was to a place where he could wade across. When he came to a rocky wall, there was always a path up it. When he came to a cliff or a crevice, his path always led him safely around. The thing always stayed with him, unseen in the shadows. Finally, the sunrise provided a dim light so that he could see the thing, now only a few steps from him. It was a huge lion. The man stammered out, "Are you going to kill me?" The lion gave a low, rumbling laugh and said, "Kill you? Gracious no. I'm the one that has been leading you." Pointing with his raised paw, he said, "There is the village you're seeking."

There is a lion in the shadows leading us through the uncertainties of the day, through the looting and rioting in our major cities, through the military fears of nuclear warfare, through the pervasive political corruption, through the secular atheism that threatens to engulf our youth, through the stature-desecration and rewriting of our history, through the transgender craze, through the destruction of marriage. There is a lion moving in the darkness of our culture in whom we may place our confidence. He is called the Lion of Judah, and he will not be defeated!

We are that desperate man making a frantic and treacherous journey at night to a neighboring village. He made it safely through many pitfalls to arrive at his destination in the early morning light. He had traveled with the terrifying awareness that something ominous traveled in the darkness with him. To his surprise, he discovered at the journey's end that his companion was a huge lion, who, rather than seeking to harm him, actually was his guide.

We are on a treacherous journey through cultural pitfalls that can be life-threatening. But we have our lion! The Lion of Judah shows the way, and he cannot be defeated. His purposes in history will be accomplished. We know that statement is true both from biblical history and through numerous examples from human history. We especially see it in times of extreme trouble for God's followers.

This image is personally comforting to me, but I do not in any way take it as a promise that I nor any of my loved ones or friends will be protected from hard and discomfiting things. Nor do I take it to mean that the United States, or even democracy in general, will be protected from destruction. To my mind, it is a promise that God and His plan will emerge victorious regardless of the events that history will bring.

His promise is that God's people and His work on the earth will never end in defeat. He told His disciples that "the gates of hell will not withstand the power of my church" (Matthew 16:18). Jesus was not speaking about any particular social organization (normally referred to as "denominations"). His church is made up of all persons who have committed themselves to (have faith in) Jesus. The Greek word for church is *ecclesia*, which means "called-out ones." His church is made up of every person who has heard His call and His invitation and responded with a heart-felt and life-changing "Yes!" This church will never be overcome (defeated, destroyed, retreating in disarray) by the open gates of Hades. That is God's promise.

That church can know at least one thing for sure: Our lion is with us today. Proverbs 30:29–30 tells us that a lion is stately in his stride. He is "mighty among beasts" and "retreats before nothing" (Proverbs 30:30). Our lion knows our needs and our destination in life, and he is powerful enough to provide what we need as we make our journey. In this manner, he protects his "called-out ones."

That promise unites us. For example, there was once a businessman in South Korea traveling on a city bus. The man sitting next to him was reading a small book in the Korean language. The businessman did not speak Korean, but he was fascinated that the other man was running his finger down the page (Korean is written in straight lines from the top of the page to the bottom) and mumbling under his breath at each word. At a given point, he seemed to be saying "Jesus." The businessman suddenly pointed to that character and said, "Jesus?" A huge smile crossed the face of the other as he said, "Jesus!" They sat there smiling and saying, "Jesus." Neither could speak the other's language, but they were connected by that name.

Revelation 5:5 (NLT) identifies our lion as Jesus, the Lion of Judah. It says, "Then one of the elders said to me, 'Stop weeping! Look, the Lion of Judah, the heir to David's throne, has won the victory!'" Our Lion will never go down in defeat, and neither will His people, regardless of events in history or in our personal lives. So, what do you say to that lion? You say, "God, thank you for dying for me and forgiving me and for all the many gifts you have given me. Here is my life, surrendered into your hands. Let me live courageously for you as long as I have breath."

Wonder and a Wooden Post

"We fix our gaze on things that cannot be seen. For the things we see will soon pass away, but the unseen will last forever" (2 Corinthians 4:18, NLT).

In one of my books, I included a picture of a toddler. Still in diapers (you could see them under her white pants), she was bent at the waist, stiff-legged, with her nose close to the ground. Her attention was fixed on the flower of a dandelion. I do not remember exactly what point I was making with the picture, but I know what I have thought about the picture over the years. It reminds me of that wonderful childhood capacity for interest in all of physical reality. Children have an inner dimension that enables them to see more than an outer form. The questions they constantly ask lead us to know that they sense an inner meaning, a deeper reality than what meets the eye on the surface.

Something happens to us as we grow toward adulthood. We begin to ask, what are we supposed to see? Thus, we come to the place where we see only the outer form. We only see what we saw yesterday. And then we become bored and see nothing. Sad, but true.

To put it in other words, what we lose in "maturity" is the capacity to wonder. We are surrounded every day by miracles, and we remain blissfully unaware of a single one. I give an example or two. Consider such a simple thing as seeing itself. According to Roy Varghese in *The Wonder of the World*, to match the retina's processing power, "a robot vision program would have to perform 1,000 million computer instructions per second." Millions of chemical changes and electrical messages have happened in your head and eyes as you read the words of this paragraph. Miracles?

Or how about digestion? How does my body take energy originating in the fiery furnaces of the sun and convert it from an apple in which it is stored into the energy I use to blink my eyes? Or walking. It seems such a simple thing. But how many muscles and internal organs must the brain coordinate with how many millions of chemical transformations does it require for us to take a single step? Every day, we are covered up with miracles, and they are so close we cannot see them. We see the outer forms and fail to "see the unseen."

We who live in the deep piney woods of East Texas are most blessed. Abundant rainfall and rich, fertile soil have given us some of the most awesome natural surroundings right here in our backyard. There are a few hilly miles of Highway 259 north of our city just before leaving our county that are simply awesome. Or, if you prefer a vista, try Highway 7 just north of Swift. The road mounts a hill at the top, of which you see many miles of a wooded valley. One can view this same scene from several hilltops that can only be reached on horseback. I could go on, but you get the point, I'm sure. Every neighborhood, like ours, is crammed with awe-inspiring scenes.

As we encounter these places, we can either *see* them or not. Many of us have become so jaded with our fast-paced lives that we simply do not see what is around us. But if we do choose to see, our eyes may open us to reality at one of three levels: 1) We can simply see the physical forms. "I am looking at hardwood and pine trees." 2) We can see the awesome beauty of that reality. Singled out, some of those trees are breathtaking in their size and spread. When we are filled with wonder at the startling beauty of creation, we are taking the first steps of "seeing the unseen." 3) This third level is what it is all about. When creation overwhelms us and fills us with awe, we become aware of a presence. Someone is there who designed and brought all reality, including us, into existence. Physical reality shows us the face of God. When God finished each day's work (whatever a "day" was), He said that it was good (Genesis 1:9–12). When He finished everything, the Bible says, "God saw all that he had made, and it is very good" (Genesis 1:31). The important word for our purposes today is "saw." God saw it. I am sure that He appreciated its outward beauty and its order and the creativity of it all. But it was "very good," not just because it shows God's creativity and artistic skill. It was good because God put His own reflection in it.

The Greek word *cosmos* is used as a designation of the universe. Originally, the Greek word meant "to arrange in an orderly fashion." We get our English word "cosmetics" from that same source, and it means "to enhance or to adorn." The universe is God's work of enhancement or adornment. Indeed, it is His masterpiece. But it is awesome because it reveals the beauty, imagination, and creativity of God. The psalmist states, "The heavens declare the glory of God" (Psalm 19:1). Paul declares, "Through everything God made, [we] can clearly see his invisible qualities––his eternal power and divine nature" (Romans 1:20).

Jesus was particularly adept at seeing the reality within (or, perhaps I should say beyond) the physical form. He did not see only sparrows; He saw trust in God (Matthew 6:26). He did not see blossoms only; He saw glory and splendor greater than anything Solomon ever possessed (Matthew 6:28–29). When He saw a farmer broadcasting His seed, He saw the many ways humans receive the Word of God (Mark 4:1–9). When He saw loaves broken to be eaten, He saw His body broken for us (Luke 22:19). When He saw the cross, He did not see his death; He saw the life He desires to give to us. He opened physical reality so that He saw in everything the dazzling truth of God and His love for us.

Jesus saw beneath the outer form of persons. For example, when approached by the Roman centurion asking for help with his paralyzed and suffering servant, Jesus did not see a military officer. The centurion was a hated enemy, a member of an offensive occupying army, and not just a member of that army, but a leader. Jesus saw none of that. He saw the inner turmoil of a hurting human being in need (Matthew 8:13). When He saw Matthew, He did not see a corrupt tax collector. He saw a hurting and searching man who would later write the story of His life (Mark 2:13–17). When they flung the scarlet woman taken in the very act of sexual immorality at His feet, He did not see the outer form. He saw a woman in need (John 8:1–11). Or, the widow who gave only two pennies. Others saw a useless old woman; He saw one who gave her all (Mark 12:41–44).

That is what we miss when we see only the outer forms of the people and things that surround us. We miss the presence. It is not that we study nature and then we can make a list of things we know about God. (You could come to my house and look around for a while and make a pretty accurate list about me, but only when I am present will you know me.) We can see the physical beauty of creation and be filled with admiration but fail to be aware of the presence. If so, we have missed the unseen, and it is only in the unseen that truth is found. And only there do we encounter God in the universe.

The inspiration for this essay came from an article G. K. Chesterton wrote in 1936, entitled "Wonder and a Wooden Post." He knocked his head against a wooden post while walking in a garden one day. He began to examine the post, which he had failed at first to see. It was real: it was there. He was surprised to see that the color and the grain of the wood and its sturdiness all came together to be beautiful! He was "seeing the unseen." Maybe the place where God has put us on earth can become our post, knocking us on the head to show us God! You think?

The Tyranny of Freedom

Somewhere long ago, perhaps as a teenager or certainly in my twenties, I read this sentence: "Human beings are cursed with the freedom to choose." I don't remember the book, but

I have never been able to shake the impression that sentence made on me as a seriously religious person. I had always thought of freedom as a blessed gift. After all, didn't Jesus say that "the truth will make you free"? God has given us freedom. How can we associate that gift with being "cursed"?

It is true, of course, that God gives us freedom. We are created "free moral agents." As humans, we are not ruled entirely by instincts as other animals are. We have free will. The Bible is filled with the assertions that we have the ability to make judgments about our behavior and freely decide how we want to live. A few examples: After forbidding the eating of the fruit of a specific tree, God walked away and left the first pair to obey or not. They were on their own and would live with whatever decision they freely made (Genesis 2:15–17).

God, through Moses, declared, "Today I am giving you a choice. You can choose life and success or death and disaster" (Deuteronomy 30:15, CEV). Joshua told the people, as he was preparing to surrender leadership, "Choose you this day whom you will serve" (Joshua 24:15).

Jesus' invitation was to "whomsoever will, let him come" (John 3:16). His invitation is to all people everywhere. The decision to accept or reject the invitation is up to each one. He invites, "Come to me all of you who are weary and carry heavy burdens" (Matthew 11:28, NLT). This offer of help is open-ended. But again, there must be a decision to accept. He stands at the door and knocks, but we must open the door (Revelation 3:20). Finally, the New Testament closes with the words, "Come…, let the one who desires take freely of the water of life" (Revelation 22:17). There can be no doubt that the Scriptures tell us that God has given to each one the gift of free will.

As a lifelong teacher, I have always held that there are two minds involved in learning: the teacher's mind sends out a message, and the mind of the student must reach out and take the message in. One is the sender, and his task is important. He must clearly understand what he purports to communicate, and, in my perspective, he is responsible for presenting the material in an interesting and clear manner. But the task of the receiver is equally as important. He has the responsibility to concentrate, carefully consider, and then make a part of his own understanding and knowledge that is communicated. The teacher, if he is worthy of the name, *must* do his job. He has no choice. But the student is free. He can refuse to learn. That he is free to choose demonstrates the burden (the cost) of freedom!

It is in this sense that we may correctly connect being free with being cursed. Freedom, it turns out, is not free. That is, it comes with responsibilities. Every decision, regardless of its size or significance, has consequences. Ralph Waldo Emerson was the first to say, and many others have quoted him (most without giving credit), "Sow a thought, reap a deed. Sow a deed, reap a habit. Sow a habit, reap a character. Sow a character, reap a destiny."

A choice is not just a choice. We don't just choose between two (or more) alternatives about a single act. We are not simply asking, "Do I do this or not?" Making a decision is much more complex. We are deciding the course of our life from that day on because a choice makes something permanent in us. Each decision leaves its imprint on us.

Let me give you an example from my life. When I was twenty-three, fresh from receiving a master's degree, I was taking the Miller's Analogy Test to begin further graduate studies. This test measured not only knowledge or information level; it also evaluated a person's ability to think. The questions were in a thin booklet, and we were given two pages of answer sheets. The answer sheets were arranged in such a way that when I turned to the second page, I saw the correct answers to four questions at the bottom of the first page. I had answered incorrectly in every case.

I faced a dilemma. I greatly desired to get into that program of graduate study. And passing that test was an important step in that direction. Who would know if I changed those answers to help my final score? Who would it hurt? I ached with the temptation to change my answers. However, I was applying to a program of graduate study in Greek and New Testament. How could I cheat in order to study the Bible? I left the answers unchanged (and I got in, and I finished the program).

My point in this little story is that my decision that day made an impact on my life. I have often wondered how my life would have been different if I had followed my temptation to cheat. What rationalizations would I have had to make in order to justify my decision? Would I have found it easier to cheat in other ways? Or, would I have become a rigid moralist always condemning "cheaters"? (This dysfunction is often the response of those who feel guilty about some unethical choice. They become an unbending opponent of those who do, or who are even tempted to do, the very thing they themselves have done.)

Jesus said that the kingdom He invites us to enter is like a treasure hidden in a field (Matthew 13:44). We who accept that invitation are ecstatic with joy at our discovery. It is interesting, in that regard, to remember that Paul told Timothy to "guard the treasure that has been entrusted to you" (2 Timothy 1:14). Jesus has called us to a "way" of living.

Do not be confused. He has not given a list of rules to be checked off each day. The path of faith is a *path*, a way of going. It is principles that guide our choices. And it is not debatable. We cannot follow if we are to walk the path to which He calls us. He clearly says it is a narrow and difficult path (Matthew 7:13–14). We have been entrusted with a precious treasure that is heavy to bear. It is frequently counter-intuitive and nearly always different from what our human nature would desire. Guarding that treasure is very frequently tough.

Even a Christian can refuse to follow. Jesus' invitation to enter the narrow gate was made to His disciples (Matthew 5:1). We can choose to stay immature and remain just like the rest of the world. That is our choice. But to refuse to enter that unseen kingdom is to miss the joy.

I love Garth Brooks' song from a few years back called "The Dance." The chorus contains the line, "I could've missed the pain, but I would've missed the dance."[13] One way would have allowed me to miss the hard spots. But that way would also have deprived me of the joys. The point is we are free to choose, and that is our curse.

Does God Have a Funny Bone?

"The one who sits enthroned in heaven laughs" (Psalm 2:4).

I think that God is happy and that He laughs a lot. I know this because humans can laugh. And I know that we have no

---

13 Brooks, Garth. "The Dance." *Garth Brooks*. 1989.

positive trait which God does not have. After all, we were created in God's image. Our sense of humor and ability to laugh are among our most wholesome and healthy traits. We share these qualities with God. The halls of heaven must ring with laughter.

I was first introduced to this idea in 1966 when I read a book by the Christian philosopher Elton Trueblood entitled *The Humor of Christ*. Frankly, when I first saw it in a bookstore, the title surprised me. I had always seen Christianity and the Bible as deadly serious business. In my thinking, Jesus was solemn, sober, and had no time for anything that was not entirely momentous. No fooling around with funny stuff. Trueblood's book changed my mind.

Erma Bombeck tells in one of her books about a "church lady" who told her, "We know Jesus never laughed because the Bible does not say he did." Bombeck's response: "Neither does it say that he wet his pants, but if he was ever two years old, we know he did." Actually, Bombeck was right, and the church lady was wrong. The New Testament bristles with references to Jesus' humor. Think about the nicknames He gave His disciples. He called James and John, reticent and introverted brothers, "sons of thunder," which could be translated as "sons of commotion" (Mark 3:17). And when He named the impetuous, overeager Simon "the rock" (Matthew 16:18), can there be any doubt that there was a smile on His face? I bet a gentle laugh passed through the disciples themselves, including "the rock."

Or, how about some of the word pictures He created? For example, the blind leading the blind and both falling into a ditch (Matthew 15:14). Or the rich man and the eye of a needle (Mark

10:25). Only a foolish man puts a lamp under a basket (Matthew 5:15), or builds his house on sand (Matthew 7:26). The people of His day would not have missed the humorous irony in these pictures. How can we?

Jesus also used wordplay that is apparent in an English translation but much clearer in the original Aramaic. For example, in Matthew 23:24, He chides the Pharisees, "Blind guides, you strain out a gnat but swallow a camel." We get the general idea, and it is funny. But it is even more powerful in the language Jesus spoke. The word for "gnat" in Aramaic is *gamia*, while the word for "camel" is *gaima*. No doubt this bit of wordplay would have brought a happy smile to the faces of the original listeners.

It should not surprise us that Jesus was a man of laughter. His Father in heaven also has a robust sense of humor. Let me give only two pieces of evidence for this statement. Consider His creation. Only a genuine sense of humor would allow God to create the duck-billed platypus. This little animal, shaped much like an otter, is an egg-laying mammal whose lips are the size and shape of a duck's bill. It can live burrowed underground or in the ocean. About the size of a coon, it has very short legs that allow it to move extremely fast in water or on the ground.

Or consider the proboscis monkey. Weighing only a few pounds, this little mammal has a very small head with huge eyes and very large ears that stick up like the ears of a German shepherd. It is nocturnal and extremely timid. Further, the deep underwater world is populated with creatures that are strange-looking, to say the least. Insects like wasps, grasshoppers, and ladybugs are not only fascinating and beautiful but are comical in how they live. God's creation is crammed with overwhelming evidence that He is joyful and fun-loving (to be totally frank, I often realize that when I look in a mirror).

My second piece of evidence that God has a sense of humor comes from a consideration of my two dogs. Rachel and I have two mutts we got at the pound, each weighing about fifteen pounds. They are fed their evening meal at 3:30 p.m. At about 2 p.m., they begin all kinds of tricks to make us think that it is time to eat. They do that every day without fail. We find their antics genuinely funny, and we laugh a lot at their efforts. Don't you think God must be similarly amused by our efforts to manipulate Him? Surely, He must see our clumsy efforts to wring from Him what we want (I have even said to God, "I want this for your glory, not for my benefit!"). Heaven must be filled with laughter.

I hope this writing has not appeared sacrilegious or irreverent. I know that God is the creator, redeemer, and judge of the earth and all that is in it. We are dealing with a God described in Hebrews 12:9 as a "consuming fire." God is an awesome force that asks us to follow a way of life that goes against the grain. It is not easy to be what God calls us to be if we take Him seriously.

In this connection, I think of my earthly father, who was an awesome man for me. To be the man he taught me to be was not easy. Yet I wanted to be that man (and I still do), not because of fear of his punishment. Rather, I did not (and still do not) want to disappoint him. That is what Hebrews 10:31 (ESV) means when it says, "It is a fearful thing to fall into the hands of a living God."

I guess I must confess that I really *want* God to have a sense of humor. I love to laugh, and I also know that humor and gentle teasing are methods of using words to establish a healthy connection. We may call that connection friendship, intimacy, closeness, fellowship, whatever. The point is humor is an important way, not the only one but a significant way, to connect us to other humans. Would it not be surprising that God, who seeks a relationship with humans, would create us with a funny bone and He Himself be without one?

Humor and gentle teasing are methods of using words to establish a connection. My dad taught me a lot in this category. My dad was always teasing other people. There was always laughter when he was around. I had noticed, however, that there were some people that he did not tease. One day, when I was about fourteen, I asked him about that. His answer taught me a lot about humor and about my dad. He said, "I only tease people I like." He went on to explain to me exactly what I am trying to say in this essay. Our words establish connections. Doesn't it make sense that a vital method of connecting with God is laughter?

Proverbs 17:22 tells us that a merry heart is a good medicine, while a crushed spirit dries up the bones. Laughter is good for us. Studies show that laughter increases the flow of oxygen to the heart and brain, among many other positive physical effects. Also, laughter increases our closeness to others, which is good for our emotional health. Finding reasons to laugh, especially at ourselves, helps us live longer and enjoy the days of our lives more. So, let us pray, "God, give us a sense of humor like yours. Please help us learn to laugh like you."

The Thread

"I will instruct you and teach you the best path for your life; I will counsel you and watch over you" (Psalm 32:8).

God is notorious for calling people to get up and move without telling them their destination. It seems to please Him to send us forth without our knowing exactly where we are going. Look at what He said to Abram, the newlywed. "Leave your country, your people, and your father's household, and go to a place I will show you" (Genesis 12:1). When Isaiah responded to God's call, the Lord simply said, "Go and preach..." (Isaiah 6:8–9).

Basically, He did the same with Jeremiah. After assuring Jeremiah that He knew him before he was formed in his mother's womb, God said, "You must go wherever I send you to and say whatever I command you" (Jeremiah 1:7). To Amos, God said simply, "Go, prophesy to my people Israel" (Amos 7:15). Although Amos was a farmer and shepherd of a flock in the southern kingdom of Judah, God sent him into the strange land of the northern kingdom called Israel. He gave him no instruction of where exactly to go nor what to say. It seems that God follows that model in dealing with those who are closest to Him throughout the Old Testament.

Jesus does the same. His original invitation to His disciples was, *"Come follow me"* (see, for example, Mark 1:16–17). When blind Bartimaeus called out for help, Jesus responded, "Come here." Only when the blind man had made his way through the crowd to where Jesus stood did he receive his sight (Mark 10:46–52). Once, two men whom He had just met asked Him,

"Where do you live?" He replied, "Come, and you will see" (John 1:38–39).

The major point is obvious. It takes faith, deep and courageous faith, to live a Christian life in a world of such uncertainty as we face today. But how, when we are puzzled about what to do next, does God keep His many promises like the verse quoted at the beginning of this essay? He assures us, not once but multiple times, that He will show us the best path for our life. How? Are we abandoned to our rationality, our education, our feelings, our desires, our IQs, and advice from friends to figure it out for ourselves? Yes and no! We have these things, and they are considerable tools. So, yes, we can use all of them. But no. We are not abandoned. Because we belong to Him, we trust and want to serve him; we have a deeper reality to show us the path.

William Edgar Stafford (died 1993) wrote an intriguing poem that addresses that deeper reality. He called the poem "The Thread." He said that there's a thread you follow, and it weaves itself among things that change. But it doesn't change. And as you hold it, you feel lost, and all the bad stuff of life happens—tragedies, pain, death, old age, whatever. But as long as you hold the thread, you cannot get lost. Nothing you do can stop the movement of time. But you don't ever let go of the thread.

I can relate to this poem. Everything does change. Suffering, old age, and death are real. (There is also joy, peace, friendship, and love along the way.) And, as a believer, I can relate to that thread that keeps me from getting lost in confusion. For me, the thread is the "presence of God" promised in the Scriptures innumerable times. This real presence is most often referred to as "the Holy Spirit" and is always described in terms of the power of God acting in the world.

Most of us are familiar with the story of Joseph in the Old Testament. Sold into slavery in Egypt, he became the servant of Potiphar, a high-ranking official in the Egyptian government. He rose to a most trusted position in Potiphar's household. But he was condemned by the false accusations of Potiphar's wife and was thrown into prison. Here is the description of that reality in Joseph's life as he lands in the dingy and unsanitary conditions of an Egyptian prison. But while he was there in the prison, Yahweh was there with him (Genesis 39:20–21). There is the thread. God was with him.

So, okay, I can understand the words. But I am still asking, how can I know the presence of God in my life? How does God as a spirit communicate with me as a flesh and blood human being? How do I experience God as my guide in the midst of the changes Stafford mentions? As a partial answer to those questions, I would like to offer a single, simple suggestion that is not often thought of in connection to God's guidance in our life. And I would like to use my own experience as an example.

God makes use of our discomfort and dissatisfaction. Sometimes, God guides us by allowing us to find our way by our own discomfort. Our uneasiness makes us wonder if we are doing something wrong that we must change or if, perhaps, we are in the wrong place. Two events in my life when I was twenty decided the pattern of my entire life. The first was in a college classroom. I was seriously considering becoming a medical doctor. The degree plan I was following put me in an anatomy class. I greatly enjoyed the lectures. Not so much the lab work. In the lab, I was assigned one day to take the heart from a living frog, hook it to a machine, bathe it in a liquid, and keep it beating for two minutes. Later, I was given a cadaver of a skinned cat and instructed to dye all nerves on one side with a blue color. I changed my major! But I had no idea where to go.

The second experience came a few weeks later on a Saturday morning on my knees in a Sunday School classroom at my church. I was nailing down hardwood flooring with Mr. Rabb, an older member of our church whom I respected greatly. I don't remember what we were talking about as we worked. But somewhere in that conversation, Mr. Rabb said to me, "Jimmy, I see you as a teacher." Those words stuck; they removed the discomfort, and here I am, sixty-four years later, after a lifetime as a teacher. My discomfort with a frog's heart and a dead cat led me to listen to Mr. Rabb. God at work, you think?

One thing I can say for sure. God will seldom communicate with us in ways we expect. What we would like is that God would say, "Okay, I am going to tell you the plan. Here is exactly where we are going and what is going to happen to you on the way. Also, you will know precisely why each thing happens." I'm afraid not. God's guidance is more like the headlights on your automobile. They do not allow you to see from where you are all the way to your destination. They shine a hundred yards down the road, and as you drive, they move ahead to supply another hundred yards.

And to cap it all off, God always gives us a sense of peace when we follow Him. But, be aware peace does not always mean a lack of fear and some degree of uncertainty. I have been fearful many times when the risks were high. But there has always been a deeper sense of peace despite the fear. That peace is the Holy Spirit at work.

Pseudo-Dionysius, the Areopagite, Christian philosopher and theologian in the sixth century, spoke beautifully of that thread. He called it a chain attached to heaven and said, "We begin our spiritual journey thinking we are pulling on the chain. As we make our path through the years, we realize that the chain is pulling us." We think we are holding the thread when, all the while, the thread (God) is holding us!

One last thing. God is pleased with us when we, by faith, walk a path not knowing the destination. The New Testament describes Abraham with these words: "By faith Abraham, when he was called to go to a place that he would later receive as an inheritance, obeyed and went even though he did not know where he was going" (Hebrews 11:8). Abraham held tightly to the thread and went where it pulled, and today, we remember him with respect and honor. I suppose no one would have blamed him if he had not. But if he had not, no one would even know his name.

The Day Jeremiah Bought the Brooklyn Bridge

"And I bought the field at Anathoth from Hanamel, my cousin, and weighed out the money to him, seventeen shekels of silver. I signed the deed, sealed it, got witnesses, and weighed the money on scales" (Jeremiah 32:9–10, ESV).

One can only express surprise at Jeremiah purchasing a field from his cousin. Jeremiah is the epitome of practicality. He carefully considers the meaning of the words he chooses to express the message God gives him. He sees how impractical it would be for him to take a wife and raise children with God's awesome calling resting on his shoulders. He is a prudent, careful, wise man. Yet, he buys a field, and we shake our heads in shock. He appears to be an impractical fool, not unlike the sucker who buys the Brooklyn Bridge from a street-smart con man. It is not the purchase that surprises us; it is the time when he made the purchase.

Zedekiah, the king, in a foolish act of desperation, attempted to negotiate a pact with Egypt as protection from Nebuchadnezzar, king of Babylon. Twice before, this powerful king had invaded Judah and taken captives back to Babylon (605 and 595 BC). His patience had run thin with Jerusalem, and he and his overwhelming army had destroyed other Judean cities and now were poised to take the holy city. Jeremiah repeatedly warned Zedekiah that Jerusalem would fall and the Babylonians would destroy the city and everything in it.

It is at this point that Jeremiah buys his cousin's land. He carefully measures out the agreed-upon price (about seven ounces of silver, not an exorbitant price) and has the deed signed and recorded according to law. It is possible that he had never seen the land he bought. We know that he never planted a tree on it nor dropped a seed of any kind in its soil. Neither did he graze a single sheep or goat on it nor carry a pail of water to irrigate so much as one plant. In fact, it is possible that Nebuchadnezzar's army was camped on that very spot when he bought it.

What was going on in the mind of this wise and prudent man? He answers that question with a beautiful statement recorded in Jeremiah 32:15. He says, "This is what the Lord Almighty, the God of Israel says: Houses, fields, and vineyards will again be bought in this land." Jeremiah offers an inspiring prayer to God, thanking Him for the Exodus and bringing his people into this land. Then he gives witness to God's promise, "I will bring them back to this place and let them live in safety. They will be my people and I will be their God" (Jeremiah 32:37–38).

When he buys the land, Jeremiah declares, "This is not the end. This is God's continued work with His people to bring redemption to humankind. There is a future, and I am making an investment in that future." Jeremiah knew that the Babylonian army could not destroy the plans of God. That army is, in fact, a tool in the hand of God to bring about His plan.

Jeremiah knew, despite the bleak outlook of the devastation to come, that this was not the end of God's purposes for his people. God had made a covenant with Abraham and his seed to bless them and to use them as a blessing to the nations. God will keep His word. Jeremiah knew that. The children and grandchildren of those captured and taken into slavery in Babylon would return to re-form God's people through whom God would bless all nations.

Buying that land was a sign of hope. Jeremiah trusted God despite the everyday events around him. Hope recognizes the reality of the situation but is not confined to that reality. Hope is aware of a reality beyond the physical circumstances. Life is going somewhere. We are people on the way, and that means there is a future. Faith combined with hope places that future in the hands of God. Therefore, life is constantly moving toward a destiny, a goal, and a purpose under the guidance of the hand of God.

It would be hard to think of a darker night in the history of Israel than the one the nation faced in Jeremiah's time. They had turned their back on God and appeared on the verge of extinction. Soon, the temple, the place where God met the people, would lie in rubble, and all able-bodied persons would be enslaved in Babylon. The end seemed just around the corner. But Jeremiah saw a shaft of light in the darkness shining on the hand of God.

Can we? Are we modern-day Jeremiahs living through the darkest night of our country? Is our faith robust enough to hope for God's hand in our darkness? Ours, like Judah, is a spiritual problem. Many in our land, our kinsmen like Jeremiah's cousin, have given up. They want to sell their land and escape, so to speak. Do we have what it takes to buy their piece? We buy when we live the Christian life openly expressing our faith in our God. That is where Jeremiah placed his trust. "It is not by power or might, but by my spirit, says the Lord Almighty" (Zechariah 4:6). Can we trust God to bring it back? Our part is to live our faith and hope. Jeremiah says to God time and again, "Nothing is too hard for you" (Jeremiah 32:17).

Christian hope that can sustain us is a reliance on grace in the face of troubling circumstances. We receive life as a gift, not as something we deserve nor as a reward for our goodness. It comes from the amazing love of God, and it gives hope in times of trouble, allowing us to live in dark nights patiently, expectantly, resiliently, and joyously in the efficacy of the Word of God. We buy property when we pray lovingly and sincerely for this great country that has blessed us. We buy property when we live to serve Him and love others with everything we have. We buy property when we give our money, our time, our courage, our words of encouragement and inspiration. We buy property when we ask God to help us live the Christian life to the fullest.

We must hear and respond appropriately to what God says. Our acts may rarely be spectacular. They will largely go unnoticed, and when they come to our culture's attention, they may be judged to be impractical or even devious. We may be shunned or ridiculed. But, and this is the point, as Jeremiah predicted for his nation, our children and grandchildren and great-grandchildren will plow these fields, sow their seed, plant orchards and vineyards, and graze their sheep and goats on this good land. Our actions of faith and hope may save this land for those we love most. Nothing else will.

On Being a Pilgrim and Sojourner

"You are a chosen people, a royal priesthood, a holy nation, belonging to God…. I urge you as pilgrims and sojourners in the world to abstain from sinful desires which war against your souls" (1 Peter 2:9; 2:11).

We are passing through a religious revolution in America today. For many generations, there was a common Christian culture that provided a widely accepted foundation for our society. Not everyone lived it, and no one lived it fully, but all were aware and accepting of a common morality that acted as a guide to life. The Judeo/Christian perspective gave American citizens a framework of behavior and belief. People more or less knew the Bible story and conducted their daily lives loosely upon it.

Today, a new perspective has emerged with the speed of light. It has been called an "anti-religious religion." It sees no need for Christianity. It views our faith as an obstacle to its goals. Those who hold a biblical understanding of marriage and sexuality, as examples, have gone in the space of fewer than three decades from pillars of mainstream conviction to the media's equivalent of racists and bigots. We who hold to the traditional Christian perspective are deemed outmoded and obsolete, if not downright dangerous enemies.

For the most part, believers are ill-equipped to meet these struggles and challenges of our day. We need a manual or guide that teaches us how to combat the complex issues with which the twenty-first century confronts us. And we have one. It is found in the pages of the New Testament. I am thinking specifically of the two letters that were written by the apostle Peter. The situation he addresses is not unlike the situation we face today. The Christian faith was new and directly confronted the established Greek and Roman religions of the first century. Early believers were called atheists because they refused to bow their knees to the accepted gods of that day.

The audience that Peter addressed was under heavy persecution from religious and political authorities. Peter writes about how to withstand the accusations that were being leveled at them and how to win over their religious opponents. From that perspective, these two New Testament books present a useful and effective way to survive in an unwelcoming world.

The scripture quoted at the beginning of this essay stands at the heart of his message. Peter begins by reminding the church of that day that they "belong to the Lord." They are a "chosen people," a "royal priesthood," and a "holy nation." Jesus told His disciples, "You did not choose me; I chose you" (John 15:16, GNT). Paul tells us, "You are not your own, you were bought by a price" (1 Corinthians 6:19–20). Like the covenant God had made with Israel (Exodus 19:5), God has entered into a binding relationship with us. We are His because He bought us with a heavy price. Jesus, God Himself, died for us. He offers the privilege of a relationship of friendship and intimacy. Our part is obedience.

Frequently, the value of a thing lies in the fact that some particular person has possessed it. The baseball cap of Mickey Mantle is worth a huge sum because it was once worn by the great athlete. Clothes and hats, even automobiles, are held as priceless items in a museum in Fort Worth because they once belonged to John Wayne. Peter is telling these early Christians that they are valuable because they are God's possession, despite living in a world that despised and sought to destroy them. They may be ordinary and commonplace, but they acquire utmost value because they belong to God. So do we.

Peter calls the believers "pilgrims and sojourners." These words are significant descriptions of the Christian life. Our true citizenship is in heaven, not here in the world. A sojourner and a pilgrim are people who make a journey into an unknown or foreign country in search of a higher good that can transform life. Is this not an excellent description of Christian life on earth? As the song puts it, "This world is not my home, I am only passing through."[14] What I seek is the sacred goal of a "higher

---

14 Brumley, Albert E. "This World Is Not My Home." In *Legendary Gospel Favorites*, 1986.

good." That good is God Himself, who can transform my life as I make my way to my journey's end.

Peter then admonishes the believers to abstain from "sinful desires." While making this journey behind the lines of enemy territory, do not conform yourself to their way of life. As strangers in a strange land, we cannot accept their lifestyles and standards (or lack of standards). In Peter's time, as in ours, the church was under fire. Peter is aware "that they accuse you of doing wrong." The only effective way to refute these charges is to live lives so lovely that the charges would be seen as obviously untrue.

Whether we like it or not, every Christian is a highway billboard advertising Jesus. Throughout our lives (our attitude, our morals, our personality, our consistency), we either draw people toward or shove them away from our faith. Peter encourages his readers in the first century to live "good lives among the pagans" (1 Peter 2:12). The word he uses for "good" is *kalos*, which means "lovely." Peter is saying that we must make our way of life so lovely and so upright that any accusation made by our enemies would be demonstrably false.

It is of interest to note that Roman and Christian historians of the first through fourth centuries have recorded many of the slanderous accusations against Christians during those years. The list is long. The most famous description of this systematic attack against Christians was made by Celsus, a second-century Greek philosopher and outspoken opponent of Christianity. He accused Christians of many things: ignorance, foolishness, superstition, but *never of immorality.*

Eusebius, a fourth-century Christian historian, would write that by his time, these slanderous attacks had come to an end because Christians had been "acknowledged to be superior to all in dignity and temperance." At his writing, no "such slander as our ancient enemies delighted to utter" remained. Persecutions remained, however, because Christians continued to refuse worship of Caesar. But the excellence of their lives had silenced the malicious accusations. Lovely, Christ-like lives had won the day. And they will win today.

• CHAPTER 4 •

The Path of Miracles and Unexpected Blessings

Miracles have a purpose beyond the miracle itself. We modern believers often miss that truth. God does a miracle for some purpose other than the miracle itself. The New Testament often refers to miracles as "signs." Eric Metaxas explains: "Miracles point to something beyond themselves. But to what? To God himself. That's the point of miracles—to point us beyond our world to another world." God does every miracle because He wants us to know who He is.

We often miss miracles because a miracle can be what does not happen. I remember hearing as a boy about two farmers who lived at the top of a steep hill across the road from each other. The road between them led directly into town, and at the bottom of the precipitous hill, there was a sharp right turn. One farmer excitedly told the other of something that had happened earlier that day. "My horse ran away going down that hill, and I was afraid that my wagon would turn over as we made that right turn. But we made it around safely. It was a miracle!" he exclaimed.

"Yes, it was," his friend replied, "And we can thank God for it. But remember, we have lived at the top of that hill for forty years, and never before has our horse run away. That is a miracle also." Have you ever thought that if one of your ancestors had died as a child (all the way back to Adam!), you would not be here? Thank God for the miracles of things that do not happen.

Also, we can cause miracles and unexpected blessings to happen by our choices. When we make better choices, choices closer to those of Jesus, miracles and blessings result. Try being more courteous, showing gratitude, contemplating the beautiful or awesome, offering compliments and encouragement, wearing a smile, offering to help, and being more generous. See what miracles suddenly show up in your life. A friend once told me, "I have better luck when I make better choices."

The Finger of God

"The magicians said to Pharaoh, 'This is the finger of God'" (Exodus 8:19).

Just before church about four years ago, I met my friends of several years, John and Donna Schoenrock, in the hallway just outside the church library. We stopped to visit for a few minutes. "Good news!" John said with a huge smile on his face. I was shaking hands with Donna. "What?" I said, not releasing her hand. She was smiling also. Tilting his head close to mine, he said, "There is no sign of cancer."

I still had Donna's hand in my grip, and now my left hand was gently patting our handshake. Six months before, they had been told by a team of doctors that she had a stage four, inoperable malignant tumor in her lower intestinal tract. They offered no hope for the future. Since that day, they had lived through six weeks of chemotherapy and radiation treatment, and one doctor's prediction: "This will take a miracle." They had nothing but prayer and the love of friends for support. But not now. They had been told just the week before that an MRI revealed no cancer at all. "We have been blessed with a miracle," John whispered. He had turned his head away from me so as to cover the tears in his eyes. I stood there holding Donna's hand with a sense of joy that I have felt on very few occasions. What can you say but "Thank you, God, for your love and mercy"?

"A God of might and miracle" are the words of a hymn we used to sing in church. But it seems to me that we don't see many experiences like John's and Donna's. Why is that? God loves us, doesn't He? We are His children, aren't we? Why so few miracles? Why?

I think there is a simple answer to that profound question. I think we are looking at events through the wrong eyes. Unfortunately, we see the question of miracles through the eyes of David Hume (1711–1776). For him, a secular enlightenment thinker, there is no such thing as a miracle because he understood a miracle to be "the violation of a natural law."

The universe was built on these immutable laws of cause and effect. They are changeless and, therefore, keep things orderly. (The sun always rises in the east, an unsupported object always falls to the earth, etc.) Hume said that a miracle occurs when a "god" steps in and breaks one of these laws. To Hume, this kind of thinking is fantasy and wishful thinking on the part of the ignorant and uneducated. For him, there are no miracles because these immutable and changeless laws cannot be broken.

Even Christian theologians have adapted this inappropriate and unbiblical understanding of what a miracle is. It is difficult to respond to the arguments of the unbelievers if we allow them to define a miracle from the perspective of David Hume.

As a Christian, I do not believe that the universe is run by natural laws. The cosmos is not a giant clock that God has wound up and leaves ticking on its own. God is alive in the universe, and it is He who keeps things moving in an orderly and purposeful direction. I see God as a master musician. The music He makes is the events of the world.

Think, as an example, about the hymn "What a Friend We Have in Jesus" played as a piano solo. If she chooses, the talented musician can play only the notes that are written on the page. This music is sweet and pleasing to the ear and brings us into the presence of God. But, if she chooses, as she plays those notes, she can improvise and add harmonious and inspiring tones and movements that enhance and augment the music. We still recognize the tune, but it is fuller and more meaningful.

For me, the analogy of the musician is what miracles are all about. The musician plays every note. Her fingers on a keyboard make every sound, and when she chooses, she can add something special. She breaks no rules. Indeed, she plays according to the rules. God is the giver of life, all life, and every minute of life. Every life story is "His fingers hitting the keyboard." And when He chooses, He can improvise and extend life because He is the life-giver.

In one of his tales of Narnia, C. S. Lewis introduces the Lion, his symbol for God in these stories:

> It was a lion. Huge, shaggy, and bright it stood facing the risen sun. Its mouth was wide open in song, and it was about three hundred yards away. As he walked and sang, the valley grew green with grass....

It turns out that Hume himself was looking in the wrong places. To him, a miracle was the "breaking of a natural law." He failed to see that God *is* the natural law! Notice I did not say that the natural law is God. That is "pantheism" and is a different matter. Thus, a miracle is not *breaking* the law. A miracle is God enacting what the law is supposed to do. I woke up alive this morning (a miracle). I ate a piece of toast. That is, my body took the sun's energy stored in wheat seeds and turned it into the energy I used to take a step (a bunch of miracles). I took a pen and wrote down a thought in my brain (a lump of physical matter) which, when you read, your brain (likewise a pile of physical matter) will understand (too many miracles to count).

God sings His way through the dusty valley of my life. And my life is the song He sings. Every act, including each breath I take, is His finger on the keyboard. This, I think, is what John meant when, in a later telephone conversation, he said, "We had miracles at every step of the way." The process seemed at the time to be no more than a leaf swirling and turning in meaningless directions carried along to no goal by the fast-moving stream. But each person and each event along the way was the finger of God pointing toward the next step.

Each Sunday now, four years later, I see my friends John and Donna singing in our church choir. I do not want to diminish in the least the wonder and joy at the great miracle at the end of Donna's story. The Great Musician did an awesome crescendo for His finale. But the truth is that John and Donna were covered up with miracles the whole time. We fail to see these miracles because we are looking with the wrong eyes. Let's look again!

Fifty-Two Years of Wedding Bells

On January 10, Rachel and I celebrated our fifty-second wedding anniversary. A funny story about our wedding: Two days before our wedding day, I had lifted a bale of hay into the back end of my pickup and had thrown out my back. On the day of the ceremony, I was bent over, could hardly walk, and was unable to stand. I sat in a chair, and Rachel stood by my side as we exchanged vows. She had to bend over so that I could kiss the bride. They helped me stand, and as Rachel led me out, one of the guests, with a coy tone in her voice, said, "Have a happy honeymoon." I could hear a small ripple of smothered laughter.

So began the odyssey, which has become our fifty-two-year marriage. I can say that the fond well-wisher got her wish. We did have a happy honeymoon, and, I might add, our entire marriage has been happy. I hesitate to say that it has been successful for fear of appearing boastful. But I can say that it has been an extraordinarily happy time for me. I could ask for nothing more.

When we were celebrating forty-nine years of marriage, our grandson (aged twenty-four) and his beautiful bride began their first year of marriage. I was especially aware that as we prepared to celebrate, our grandson and new granddaughter were laying the foundation upon which the structure of their marriage would be built. And, as "the foundation goes," so "goes the marriage." The combination of these two events has led me to think about marriage, and especially about the question of how to create the miracle of a successful, happy marriage.

Books have been written in an effort to answer that question. They grapple first with a prior question: what is a successful marriage? A variety of answers to that question are available. Then comes the more difficult question: how do you pull it off? No way in a brief essay like this one can hope to even begin to address these two difficult and important questions.

But there is one thing I can do. There is a single factor that I think is *the* necessary ingredient. It is the *sine qua non* ("that without which") no marriage can be happy. Without this quality, one may perhaps have a marriage that may be called "successful," depending on how success is defined. (One may, as an example, say that a marriage that does not end in divorce is a successful marriage. A most impoverished definition, in my thinking.) But I can say, without fear of contradiction, that without the quality I have in mind, no marriage can be happy. And with it, happiness is guaranteed!

I learned about this quality one summer about thirty years ago while I was teaching in Israel. One of my students brought me a little hardbound book written by a man named Hiam Friedman. He was an eighty-five-year-old rabbi who had been married to a woman named Rachel for sixty years. The book was entitled *How to Have a Successful Marriage*. That title intrigued me, especially when written by a man who had been married to the same woman for sixty years. My thinking was that any man who had managed to stay married for that long and then write a book about it must have something good to say.

I was right. It was an excellent little book, well-written with very helpful ideas. A single line reached out from the page and grabbed my attention, and it has never left my mind since I read it. Rabbi Friedman said, "God created me to help Rachel become all that God intended her to be." Wow! Here was a man who had served as a great rabbi, training hundreds of young men and women to serve God. He had raised several children to be responsible adults. He had courageously served his country through very trying times. He had written several good books that would influence generations. But he named none of these significant accomplishments as the primary reason God had created him. God created him, he said, primarily to help a specific woman fulfill her potential.

Rabbi Friedman did not say, or I don't remember if he did, that such an attitude must be reciprocated. Both husband and wife must take this attitude toward the meaning of marriage. Can you see how a marriage built on this principle would offer nothing but happiness to both partners?

Please do not misunderstand. I am not saying that a husband's happiness is built exclusively around knowing that his wife is there to help him. He knows that he has his wife's support, of course, and that gives him comfort and strength. What I am saying is that his happiness comes from helping her toward her potential. It brings him happiness to know that, at the deepest level, his life is meaningful as he supports and encourages her to be what God intended her to be. And that also is true for the wife. To paraphrase the old saying, what is good for the gander is good also for the goose.

That, in fact, is the definition of love in any context. I see you as an "unfinished product," a "being on the way," a fact true of all of us throughout life. And I resolve to be with you in such a way as to help you achieve that potential. I do not define the potential; that is your job. Rather, I offer support and encouragement. Of course, that resolution to help comes at differing levels. For example, a teacher does that with a student, while a father does that with his child. The resolution is the same regardless of the situation. What varies is the duration and the intensity. It is love in action, in any case.

I see this principle when God created marriage. Immediately after creating the two sexes, God says, "For this reason a man will leave his father and mother and be united to his wife and they will become one flesh" (Genesis 2:24, BSB). I find it surprising that God said, "One flesh." Why not "one heart" or "one soul" or even "one being"? There is a meaningful principle here. I instinctively protect my flesh. I see that it is fed, it is clean, it is clothed. I seek to keep it alive and well and to have what it needs. When we care for each other like we care for our own flesh, we find supreme happiness because that is what God created marriage for. And that is God's primary purpose in creating you and your spouse. Isn't that a wonderful path to walk through life? Yes!

The Star of Bethlehem

Matthew 2:1–12 contains the only reference in Scripture to the Magi coming from the East to visit the newborn king. Matthew gives few details in his story. But these "wise men" have captured the imagination of Christians down through the ages, and we have been ready to fill in the gaps. There were three of them, we say (probably because there were three gifts), and we have given them names: Melchior, the oldest and the leader of the group; Balthasar, swarthy and black-bearded; and Caspar, the youngest and a brilliant young scholar. They rode camels and were dressed in kingly robes and heavily adorned hats. They and their camels were present in the stable along with the shepherds and other animals; at least, our Christmas cards declare it so.

Matthew only says that "after Jesus was born," the Magi from the East came to Jerusalem and asked, "Where is he born king of the Jews? We have seen his star" (Matthew 2:2, ESV). After a visit with Herod, who was paranoid as usual about any threat to his throne, they were directed to Bethlehem. The star they had seen now rested over the place where the Child was. They found the Child with His mother in a "house" (Matthew 2:11), and they bowed down in worship and offered Him gifts of gold, incense, and myrrh. They then returned to their own country by another route (circling around Jerusalem so as to avoid a meeting with Herod). There ends Matthew's story of these shadowy individuals, whom we never hear from again.

Our curiosity is aroused. Who were they? Why did they make such a long and difficult trip to the land of the Jews, nondescript and unimportant people in the political structure of the Middle East? Did they accomplish their goals? Scholarly books have been written in answer to these questions. But the truth remains: these and other interesting questions like them can only be answered by conjecture.

The Magi were probably Zoroastrian priests from the land that today is modern-day Iran. Zoroastrians were well-educated, and, more than anything, they studied the stars. Having worked out a complicated understanding of the movement of the stars, they believed that the character and outlook of the individual were determined by the configuration of the stars on the night of his birth. Knowing the movement of the stars enabled one to predict the future (today, we call these ideas "astrology"). The Magi in Matthew's story became aware of a special star that had recently illuminated the entire sky. "This," they said, "we must investigate."

While the bulk of Zoroastrian priests lived in the area of modern-day Iran, there was a small outpost in Petra, a city in Jordan near the border of Israel. This group had become aware of and knowledgeable about the sacred scriptures of the Jews. Evidently, they knew the prophecies of the coming king, called the Messiah.

Zoroastrian priests were considered royalty and stood at the apex of their culture. They were politically powerful and economically rich (that explains how they so quickly got an audience with Herod and why they were treated with such deference by this shrewd and inhumane ruler). Because of their wealth, they had the capacity to make such a journey and bring with them such expensive gifts.

So, the Magi came, and they saw the baby. They bowed low in worship and gave their gifts, and they returned home, following a different route than the one that brought them there.

Here is where my imagination really gets going. I wish I could know what they thought about the Child they had seen. They had made a long, arduous, and expensive trip. Was it worth it, and why? What you are about to read is nothing more than my imaginative response to these questions.

In the annals of the history of the Zoroastrians in Petra, one may find this report written and signed by Melchior:

That first night after leaving Jerusalem, we camped about fifteen miles to the northeast in the lower regions of the Jordan Valley. As we ate our evening meal around a small campfire, we began to talk about our experience for the first time. I was the first to speak.

I was already bald, and a long, grey beard flowed gently from my chin. I was a skeptic. "This is all fantasy," I declared, my glance moving slowly from one to the other.

"My gold was wasted, as was my time. Did you see those people? Peasants, ignorant, useless!" My voice was raised, irritated, angry.

"And what will become of that useless baby? I can tell you; he is no king!" I paused to look slowly around, my eyes demanding agreement.

"I'll tell you what will happen. He'll be an ignorant, illiterate peasant just like his parents. A waste, I tell you." I fell silent, staring into the fire.

Balthasar spoke next, gently stroking his black beard. "Well," he began slowly, "I don't know." His voice was shaky, uncertain. He looked quickly at me as if to determine if his words were inappropriate.

"As a priest, I wanted to give something priestly, so I brought the incense. Something used in worship, you know. Incense. Quite expensive, you know." His repetitive words exposed his uncertainty. "Maybe it was a waste, but they did seem pious people and not at all lazy and shiftless." He paused, looking around. Then, he quickly threw a twig he had been playing with into the flame.

"Everything was clean and in place. Perhaps they will give the incense to a priest of their religion. Perhaps not. I don't know," he glanced at Caspar. "What do you think?"

Caspar, hardly more than a precocious teenager, looked up from the fire. He began slowly, his voice confident and sure. "I am aware of their scriptures that prophesy that this king is to usher in a different kind of kingdom. They seem to say that while his bloodline is royalty, he himself will emerge from an unexpected and common place."

He paused, gathering his thoughts. "And, strangely, they say he will be a 'suffering servant.' I am convinced that what we witnessed is in keeping with those ideas. Further, I know my gift of myrrh, used to embalm bodies, is more than appropriate. I will return to this land later, when he is a man, to see what happens to him."

He stood stretching his back. "As a student of the heavens, I cannot forget that star of Bethlehem." He paused, then added, "I'll check the camels before we go to sleep." He strode away into the darkness.

And he did return to that land. He visited the holy land many times over the years and kept up with the new king. His last visit came when he was about fifty. It was his last because he never came back to us. News had reached us that the young man had become a roving rabbi. Caspar announced that he must go and witness this phenomenon. (We know what I am about to report by the letters he sent to us.)

He caught up with the rabbi just as he was leaving Jericho on his way to Jerusalem. Caspar could not believe his eyes. He saw a blind man named Bartimaeus receive his sight! He then followed the crowd into Jerusalem, where the Jews were preparing for Passover. For several days, he heard the rabbi speak to the crowds, mostly sharing parables. Wonderful stuff.

He next heard that the rabbi had been arrested. Caspar was in the crowd when the rabbi came before Pilate, the Roman governor, who declared him innocent. But then he could not believe his ears. The crowd called for the release of Barabbas, a known murderer and thief. They screamed for the crucifixion of the rabbi instead!

Caspar was in the crowd that watched the slow and painful death of the young man born so long ago under that star of Bethlehem. Sad *and physically weary, Caspar turned away to pack his bags and head home. It was a disappointing end to a hopeful dream. But something made him stay. He did not know what.*

Three days later, he began to hear rumors that the young rabbi had risen from the dead! Once again, he doubted his ears. But the rumors persisted, and he hung around watching and listening. Then, one day, he heard one of the disciples named The Rock preach openly in the streets of the city. It was a most eloquent sermon. He heard The Rock appeal to the people to "believe." The Rock was calling people to entrust their lives to the crucified and risen rabbi. Once again, he thought his eyes were deceiving him. Over The Rock's head was a sudden light, like a flame of fire. "The star," he shouted, "the star of Bethlehem!" He felt his feet moving forward toward The Rock. "I shall make that commitment," he said aloud to himself. This is the last line of Caspar's letters to us. What happened to him from this point forward, we do not know.

As for me, I began to wonder if my original skepticism was unjustified. Perhaps so. I will search for those scrolls that Caspar was reading and take a look for myself.

We celebrate Christmas and, for a few days, think of Bethlehem and the Magi. Then we leave the manger and the baby and the star to return to our daily, ordinary lives. Like the Magi, we will "go home." What will we think of our visit to that baby's bedside? Will we go home "by a different route"? In other words, will our visit to Bethlehem make any difference in our lives?

I like Caspar's response. It exemplifies absolute trust in things our eyes and ears cannot understand. And it demonstrates the life-changing courage it takes to follow that star of Bethlehem. It reminds us of the miracles and blessings that await us as we walk in His light. I want that. And I bet you do, too.

Does the Bush Still Burn?

"Moses stared in amazement. Though the bush was engulfed in flame, it did not burn up.... God said, 'Take off your sandals, for you are standing on holy ground'" (Exodus 3:3; 3:5).

Moses had taken his sheep to the "far side of the Midian desert." There were mountains in that part of the desert where rainfall could produce grass for the sheep to graze. In the Midian desert itself, with less than five inches of rain annually, hardly anything at all grew. Shepherds took their sheep across the desert floor and stayed in the mountainous area with them for a month or two.

Having arrived at a grassy area, Moses was relaxing, sitting with his back leaning on a rock. As he glanced around, watching his sheep, he noticed a bush aflame. Nothing unusual about that. With temperatures and humidity so high, bushes with several dead branches often broke into flame (we today refer to that occurrence as "spontaneous combustion"). But as he watched, he saw something that was unusual. The bush was not consumed by the flame.

Moses stood to investigate. As he approached, a voice came from the flame, which terrified him. The voice commanded, "Take off your sandals, Moses, you are standing on *holy ground!*" He bent immediately and unloosed his sandals, and stood there barefooted on the hot earth that had been turned into a place of worship. The life of this shepherd would never be the same. The ground was holy because God was present.

For the Christian, there is never a time when we are not in the presence of God. That is a New Testament truth that can never be doubted. He has promised repeatedly that He would be with us to the end of the age. He sends His Spirit (Himself) to dwell in our hearts as a guide and comforter. But there are special times and places which we have set apart as sacred (holy ground) in ways that our ordinary life is not.

For some, a special time of prayer and meditation in our bedroom, offering a prayer of gratitude to God before our meals, or a special time of prayer with our family before we drive away from home for a long trip together can be a sacred moment, unlike and separated from the rest of our day. Some Christians have a special time each day when they go to their church for prayer. That is most definitely a sacred time in the presence of God. When I reach across our breakfast room table and take the hand of Rachel each morning and bow in prayer with her, I am in the presence of God in an unusual way. That time is not like the rest of my day.

Sunday is also a sacred day, unlike the other six days. It is a time of rest and worship. We go to church to worship with others. We sing songs, pray, listen to Bible readings, hear the Scriptures explained, and sing or hear sung the great anthems of our choir and orchestra. Or, we do some version of that. And we say that we are standing on holy ground because God is there. But we must ask, is He really there?

If it is true that God is really there speaking to us and hearing what we say to Him, as we say He is, these acts are sacred, and the church is holy ground. Our acts of worship, both in private and in public worship, are sacred only if we encounter a real, living God. That is, for our acts of worship to be sacred, God must be present, changing us, converting us, healing us, and saving us. If not, that is, if God is not present, impacting our lives and making us more like Jesus, our acts are no different from our ordinary life and are not sacred at all. We might as well be attending a play, going to a ball game, or fishing with our buddies on some beautiful lake.

I love the challenge which Peter gave to the Roman Christians of his day. They were facing heavy persecution under the despotic hand of Emperor Nero. Second Peter 1:3–4 reminds them that God's divine power (His presence) gives us everything we need for life *and godliness* through our knowledge of Him and that He has promised that we may be partakers in the *divine nature.*

I read these words with anticipation and encouragement. The door has been opened in me, if I so choose, to partake in the nature of God. I understand by these words that God will help me to share in His own qualities and character. That is what is going on when God is *present*. When we worship, we partake in more than the knowledge of God. Worship is more than an intellectual, rational process. If it is only that, then, when complete, the only thing that is different is our thinking about God. But it is much more. We participate in the very *life* of God, and *everything* is made different.

I once read of a man who said, "I don't go to church merely to learn. I go because something *happens*." There is great truth in that statement. But still, we must ask, "What happens?" I suggest a very brief answer to that question. What happens is a reenactment of what happened on that first Christmas night in Bethlehem two thousand years ago. God entered the world back then and became a man. Now, God comes into the world to be incarnated in me and you. By so doing, we get to partake in the divine nature!

If God is a personal being capable of speaking to us, as we profess Him to be, and if we partake in His nature and character, it follows that we can speak to Him. Sounds great, doesn't it? But that conversation, often taken for granted by His followers, is actually very scary. In his book called *Miracles*, C. S. Lewis says that we can tolerate a "domesticated God" whose life force we can use for our benefit. But a living being, a hunter, a king, not so much. We draw back from a real living being that lays claim to our allegiance, has expectations of us, and wishes to "interfere" with our lives. That God scares us.

Lewis concludes, "It is a kind of Rubicon (a famous river in Italy). One goes across or not. But if one goes across, there is no manner of security against miracles." Lewis is warning us that, like Moses, when we approach that bush and hear the voice of the living, real God and answer back, our life will never be the same. And the miracles begin (see the book of Exodus for how Moses's life changed). Yet, Sunday by Sunday, we are invited to approach that bush. If we listen, the real, living God will speak, and the healing, converting, and saving miracles will continue as God draws us into Himself. The bush still burns!

Everything Is a Gift

"...that everything gained and everything claimed follows upon something given, and comes after something gratu-

itous and unearned; that in the beginning there is always a gift."

Josef Pieper

Some say that it is Jesus' greatest story, and I would not disagree. It begins with the simple words, "There was a man who had two sons" (Luke 15:11). We know so well the part about the younger son, who, getting his portion of the inheritance, went away and "squandered his wealth in wild living." Hungry and knee-deep in a pig pen, he woke up ("came to himself") and decided to return to his father, who received him and welcomed him home.

We pay insufficient attention to the elder brother, whom we may call "the other prodigal son." Unlike his brother, he stayed home and worked hard to keep the farm going. When he discovered that the father had so lavishly received the wasting, self-centered, and profligate son back with robes and rings and a great party, he became angry. He told the father, "I slaved for you, I never disobeyed your orders. I did all this, and you have killed the fatted calf for him! You never gave me even so much as a goat."

The father, with patience and love, entreated his older son to welcome his brother back, saying, "Everything I have is yours." What is not often noticed is that, in the beginning, when the younger son asked for his part of the inheritance, the father divided the estate between both sons (Luke 15:12). The oldest, according to Jewish law, had gotten two-thirds of everything, and the younger had received the rest. Why did he seem to feel that he owed no sense of gratitude to his father?

It is true that he was a hard worker and had managed the farm without complaint in the younger brother's absence. The probability is that he prided himself on his "work ethic." He knew he was doing a good job, and he felt that, unlike his brother, he deserved everything he had received from his father. The philosophy of the elder brother is very popular today. You can hear people say, "Sure, I'm going to heaven. I am a good person." That is, I deserve heaven.

Jesus told another story that condemns that attitude. In response to "those who were confident of their own righteousness and looked down on everybody else" (Luke 18:9), He told the story of two men who went into the temple to pray. The one, a Pharisee, stood and "prayed about himself" (Luke 18:11). He proceeded to tell God how good he was, even pointing out to God that he was better than the other man.

The other man, a tax collector, stood at the back and would not even lift his eyes to heaven. He simply said, "God, have mercy on me a sinner" (Luke 18:13). Jesus concludes His story, "This latter man went home justified!" (Luke 18:14). I am sure that the Pharisee did everything that he mentioned to God. No doubt he followed the law to the letter. His failure, like the elder brother, was his pride in doing so. He did good in order to deserve what God had to give. In his mind, he had every right to point out to God all his good works.

There is a prayer I read once attributed to a famous rabbi. Like the Pharisee, he listed for God all the good which he did and all the bad he avoided. He concluded his prayer with the words, "If there are only two righteous ones left in the world, they are myself and my son. If there is only one, I am he." Perhaps this is a truly holy man when he compares himself to other men. When I compare myself to Hitler or Stalin, I come out pretty good. I do well when I compare myself to dope dealers, men who traffic in little girls for sexual pleasure, or those who make a handsome living fomenting hatred between the races. Where I don't do so well is when I compare myself to Jesus.

I am not sure that the same lessons are being taught to the young today that many of us adults were taught in our developing years. "Idle hands are the devil's workshop." Have you ever heard this statement? It was big around my house when I was growing up. My parents sincerely believed that trouble was just around the corner when you were just sitting around with nothing to do.

"Hard work never hurt anyone" was a motto my parents wanted me to follow. And I did, and I am glad. They were hard workers, and they taught me that hard work is what is good. I followed that principle at school, in the fields, when I got my first paying job, and throughout my life. Still today, every day, I look back over the hours and have a feeling of satisfaction when I can find some worthy accomplishment or two. Old habits die hard.

I benefited from my parents' teaching and example and have lived a life based on accomplishment. I worked hard, and I benefited greatly from it. But what I now know, but did not for most of my life, is that there is great emotional and spiritual danger in that approach to life. For most of my professional life, I believed that hard work was the solution to all dilemmas. I read somewhere Thomas Jefferson's statement, "I'm a great believer in luck, and I find that the harder I work the more I have of it." I would alter that statement a little. "I believe in the

Holy Spirit and the power of God, but I still rely on my own efforts for success."

I did not know how to allow the spirit or the power of God to work in my life. Because of my attitude, all the tension and anxiety fell on my shoulders. It never went away because as soon as one challenge was completed, another popped up to take its place. It took many years for me to experience "letting go and letting God." That came when, at long last, I realized that everything is a gift. There is nothing we have done from conception to this day that is not the work of God in our lives. Perhaps the screwups and failures belong to us. But even these give God openings and opportunities to bring good into our lives.

"We are God's workmanship," Paul says (Ephesians 2:10, BSB). In another place, Paul assures us, "He who began a good work in you will carry it on to completion" (Philippians 1:6, BSB). Can we truly commit ourselves to the truth of those statements? Can we combine them with the teaching of the entire Bible that God loves us with the love of a perfect father? When we can, we lose all fear for life, and we allow His Spirit in us to bring His power to our lives.

If I take the attitude of the elder brother, I think I deserve what I get. It is paid for my good work, and I have no need for gratitude. But when I see everything as a gift of God's love, my heart overflows with gratitude. I say thanks, and I love and worship this wonderful giver we call Father.

Believe Until You Receive

"Abraham believed...that God who calls...into being even things that do not exist" (Romans 4:17).

Abraham was a newlywed when God promised him that he would make of him a great nation. God promised that he would bless that nation and that he would bless the world through that nation. To augment that promise, God even changed Abraham's name. His birth name was Abram, which means "father." God's new name for him was Abraham, which means "father of nations."

Abraham was probably about twenty-five years old when God made His covenant with him. Did you know that the promise was not fulfilled until Abraham was a hundred and Sarah, his wife, was ninety years old? All those years, this righteous man and his wife lived expectantly, anticipating the birth of their firstborn. Year after year, Sarah's womb remained empty. Had God forgotten His promise? Had He changed His mind?

God's clock and His calendar do not move in a straight line like ours do. Time with God can stretch like an inflating balloon in all directions at once. Or, it may curve and slow to a snail's pace. Then, it might speed up like a bullet from a gun. Take Psalm 90:4 as an instance: "For a thousand years in your sight is like a day that has gone by, or like a watch in the night." Time is relative to God. Peter borrows this Old Testament understanding of time. He says that we need not get bent out of shape when things move slower than we think desirable. "With the Lord a day is like a thousand years and a thousand years is like a day" (2 Peter 3:8).

We humans, especially pragmatic Americans, judge God by our limited standards and become skeptical and impatient. We wonder if God's plans have been hindered in some way out of God's control, if He is punishing us for some unacceptable deed, or if He has changed His mind. After he has reminded us that with God, time is relative, Peter assures us, "The Lord is not slow in keeping his promise.... Rather he is patient, not wanting anyone to perish" (2 Peter 3:9). God knows what He is doing.

The Scriptures remind us in many places that God is faithful and may be counted on to keep His promises to the last detail. One of the clearest and most persuasive instances is Numbers 23:19 (ESV), "God is not man, that he should lie, or a son of man, that he should change his mind. Has he said, and will not do it? Or, has he spoken, and will not fulfil it?" Psalm 71:22 (NLT) reminds us, "You are faithful to your promises, O my Lord!" And Paul affirms, "The gifts and the calling of God are irrevocable" (Romans 11:29, ESV). There can be no doubt about it. The promise is that God will keep His promises.

How, then, are we to respond to the difference between God's timing and ours? Put at its simplest, our response must be that we believe until we receive. Paul actually addressed this question in wrestling with the interim between God's promise of a child to Abraham and Sarah and the birth of their son Isaac. He wrote about this issue in Romans 4:13–18. (The more modern translations, like the New Living Bible, make it easier to follow the logic of his argument.) God made His promises, and Abraham hung on for the long term by faith in God. Which God? "The God who gives life to the dead and God who calls into being even things that do not exist" (Romans 4:17).

Abraham had no Bible such as we have. He had no preacher and no one to explain to him the things of God. He was surrounded by pagan worshippers of gods of unnumbered sorts.

Abraham had come to believe that there was only one supreme God who created life from nothing simply by His command.

There is an interesting story among the rabbis of how Abram became convinced that there was one God. He had been to a neighboring city and was returning home one evening just after dark. He passed a village on a hill and, looking up, he saw lighted windows. If there was a village up there and there were houses with lighted lamps, he reasoned, there must be people who had brought it all into existence. If that is true for a village, how much more must it be true for the world around him?

Abraham saw that this God was a God who gave being to things that did not yet exist. It is not that He reassembles existing materials to make something new. He creates from nothing. Abraham believed that this God wanted to be known by humans and desired to have communion with them.

I like the way that Edward T. Welch brings Abraham's experience into our modern times. He says, "The basic outline is clear: If you throw your lot in with Jesus, everything he has is yours, even the kingdom itself. It would be impossible to ask for more. Those who imitate Abraham's faith are always pushing the last moment further out until it comes, even after physical death. Such a person is fearless." Welch's invitation is not a call to salvation. He is not inviting a non-Christian to an initial experience of faith. "Throwing your lot in with Jesus" is an appeal to believers to a deeper faith and total surrender to God's perfect will in our lives. And it shows up, like Abraham's faith, in daring obedience to God moment-by-moment till the end of life. It is that person, Welch insists, who is living a kind of faith that is "fearless."

So, we believe (trust) until we receive. Trust has always been a challenging issue for me. I have preferred to be in control of my life, even my spiritual life. Even as a young man, I could be described as a goal-oriented person. I liked setting my sights on an objective and figuring out how to accomplish the tasks necessary to make the goal a reality.

Normally, my prayers were always trying to get God to help me realize my goals. I always included pious phrases like "Your will be done" and "if it pleases You." I included carefully phrased statements about being guided by His love and how I knew that I could accomplish nothing without Him. But I wanted my goals, and I wanted Him to help me. I am confessing that, in the end, it was more about me and my goals than about Him.

I worked hard to accomplish those goals, and God blessed me despite my false piety. But as I have grown older, I have found that, for a number of reasons, many of my goals now allude me. I have to surrender more to God's will. I find myself confessing in my prayers, "I truly cannot do it without you, God." In one way, age has actually made it easier to imitate Abraham's faith. However, trust still does not come easy, and I don't like the limitations that have come with age. For me, it seems, one of the things God must bring into being before it exists is the very trust that I need. He has promised that He will do it for me, and He always keeps His promise. Ask Abraham.

The Sound of God's Voice Singing

"The Lord your God is with you, he is mighty to save, he will take great delight in you, he will quiet you with his love, he will rejoice over you with singing" (Zephaniah 3:17).

THE SOUND OF GOD'S VOICE SINGING

My favorite memories of my visits to the mountains of New Mexico invariably include nighttime campfires beside rushing streams. The water from melting snow is clear as crystal and cold as ice. The splashing water rushing over the rocky bottom that provides the stream bed makes a flowing, almost roaring, sound. It has a way of quietening one's heart with a sense of peace. Sitting by that fire and listening to the music of that fast-flowing stream brings me close to God. It is like a prayer when, instead of me speaking to God, He stoops low to call my name and sings His love to me.

Therefore, it is no surprise to me that John tells us in Revelation 1:15 that God's voice is "like the sound of rushing waters." He heard a loud voice behind him telling him to write on a scroll what he saw. The voice that gave him that instruction sounded like the music of a rushing stream. It is as if God is singing. And it is not John speaking to God; it is God speaking to John and to us. It is like my memories of New Mexico!

Singing is mentioned over 400 times in the Bible. Psalms is a songbook that contains hymns used in worship of God. These hymns call us to praise and adore our God with singing and musical instruments. To my knowledge, there is only one place in Scripture where it is God who does the singing. That is found in the tiny Old Testament book of Zephaniah. We do not pay much attention to Zephaniah. In fact, some would say that we wouldn't lose much if we did not even have his book. Not so. We would especially miss the teaching found in chapter 3.

Zephaniah was a contemporary of Jeremiah (630–585 BC) and preached a message similar to Jeremiah's. Only three chapters long, he spends the first two chapters in the blistering judgment of Judah, whom the Lord is about to send away into exile in Babylon. They have filled the temple with gods of violence and deceit (Zephaniah 1:9). They have forsaken Yahweh and have turned to worship Molech (Zephaniah 1:5). They have become a "shameful nation" (Zephaniah 2:1). According to Zephaniah, God has had it and is about to purify His nation.

It is the last chapter that draws our attention. Here, Zephaniah is a poet describing God's unending love for Jerusalem. He will never cut His people off. His fire is "jealous anger" designed to "purify." He will draw His people back to Him, and they will "bring offerings" (Zephaniah 3:10) and serve Him "shoulder to shoulder" (Zephaniah 3:9). His cleansed people will "eat and lie down and no one will make them afraid" (Zephaniah, 3:13). "The Lord, the King of Israel," will be with them! The whole chapter is a promise of God's work of redemption, reformation, and salvation.

In the middle of these words of comfort and challenge, Zephaniah lays down the reason for our hope. He describes the God "who is with us." He is the God who takes delight in us and rejoices over us with singing! God, like a father holding his child close to the bosom, gently sings the child to sleep. Or, like a mother whose child awakens in the night and is afraid in the dark, and she sits by the child's side and gently sings comfort and encouragement till the child falls asleep. It is this singing God who is our hope.

God does immensely more than comfort our fears when He sings over us. Singing, even human singing, is much more than words set to music. It does something that words alone cannot accomplish. Victor Hugo, famed French author of *Les Mi-*

sérables, *The Hunchback of Notre Dame,* and other classic novels, said, "Music expresses that which cannot be put into words and that which cannot remain silent."

There is a powerful mystery in song that can touch us at our deepest point. That is why our public worship is filled with songs and why Psalm 150:3–5 encourages us to "praise him with the sounding of the trumpet, praise him with the harp and lyre, praise him with the tambourine and dancing, praise him with strings and flute, praise him with the clash of cymbals." We are moved by music even when there are no words.

Zephaniah surrounds his portrayal of the singing God with a number of images of what happens to us when we hear the sounds of God singing. In Zephaniah 3:16, he says that we no longer let our "hands hang limp." God's music creates the power to serve Him. Paul makes the same point in his matchless description of God's grace in Ephesians 2. Everything comes by grace; therefore, we are God's "masterpiece," Paul says. That is, it is God's work that renews us. At the same time, we have to do the "good works" He ordains. There is a paradox here. God does it all, and we do it all! There is an old Southern saying, "Pray as if everything depended on God, and work as if everything depended on you!" God's singing gives us busy hands.

God's singing over us rescues the lame and gathers the scattered (Zephaniah 3:19). God heals us where we are broken. I love God's promise made in Malachi 4:2, "But for you who revere my name, the sun of righteousness will rise with healing in its wings. And you will go out and leap like calves released from the stall." The sounds of God's singing heal our brokenness and set us free from those things that bind us.

Zephaniah says that God's singing gives us "praise and honor" (Zephaniah 3:19). There is only one reference to Jesus singing found in the New Testament. It is in Hebrews 2:12. The writer of Hebrews is describing the humanity of Jesus and how He was "perfected by his suffering." Because He knows our struggles, He freely calls us "brothers," and, quoting Psalm 22:22, Jesus says, "In the presence of the congregation, I will sing your praises." On multiple occasions, Jesus ended a story by describing the praises that a businessman gives to a subordinate who has done a good job. "Well done, good and faithful servant." Is it too much for me to admit that I hope to hear those words of song from Jesus?

A number of people have commented that sometimes people are seen dancing and are thought to be insane by those who do not hear the music (it was Friedrich Nietzsche who first said this). Let this sentiment be said about us Christians. Let us dance with abandon to the sounds of God's singing even though unbelievers cannot hear the music. Jesus promised that they would think us crazy. Let them think as they will. We hear the music, and it makes all the difference.

• CHAPTER 5 •

Walking to Serve

Isaiah reports that as a young man, he saw a vision that forever changed his life (see Isaiah 6:1–8). He saw the Lord, high and lifted up, seated on a throne in the heavenly temple. Standing in the shadows of this holy vision, he saw himself in his brokenness and unworthiness. And as this starling vision unfolded before him, he heard the voice of the Lord saying, "Whom shall we send? And who will go for us?" (Isaiah 6:8). Before the reverberation of the heavenly voice left his ears, he heard himself willingly cry out, "Here am I. Send me!" (Isaiah 6:8). Then the Lord said, "Go!" (Isaiah 6:9).

It is this Isaiah who went forth to serve the Lord as prophet to the people of Judah. His message is recorded in the Old Testament book bearing his name. The first half of the book announces God's judgment of His people and the coming disaster of their defeat and enslavement. But, beginning with chapter 40, there is a definite change of tone. His message becomes a letter of hope. It is the promise of a messianic king whom he describes as a "suffering servant." Isaiah includes four beautiful poems known as "The Servant Songs."

Jesus claimed these songs and the message of Isaiah as a prophecy of Himself. In the synagogue of Nazareth, as He began His ministry, Jesus took the scroll and read from Isaiah 61:1–2. Sitting down, He said, "Today this scripture is fulfilled in your presence" (Luke 4:21). He is saying that He is the servant who suffers for the salvation of His people. Later, He said, "For the Son of Man came not to be served but to serve" (Matthew 20:28, NLT). We worship and follow a Savior who was a servant and who leads us on a path of service.

To Whom Has God Given You?

"For God so loved the world that he gave..." (John 3:16).

Jeremiah must have been a young man when God first spoke to him. Maybe in his late teenage years, certainly in his early twenties. Like all of us, Jeremiah was born into a world that he did not invent. His world awaited him. It had fixed customs, a language, material objects, weather patterns, rules of behavior and thinking—a whole way of life anticipated him. When he got here, there was a *before* into which he stepped. And God had a message for him when he arrived.

His father was a priest in a village three miles North of Jerusalem called Anathoth. He learned about God through Jewish eyes, and without a doubt, it was expected that he would follow in his father's footsteps and become a priest in that same village. But God, as he so frequently does, had different plans for Jeremiah. His name means "Yahweh hurls" or "Yahweh throws," and God is about to throw Jeremiah in a totally unexpected (and unwanted) direction.

It was in the thirteenth year of Josiah's reign as King of Judah that the "word of Yahweh" came to the young man. That would make the date 626 BC. We know nothing about the setting for God's message to Jeremiah. He could have been deep in prayer in his father's home where he lived. Or perhaps he was on a grassy knoll near his village with a blue sky above and a cool breeze on his face. Or perhaps he was striding along with a sweaty face on a dusty road with the sun blazing down on his shoulders. But wherever he was, God got through to him. Jeremiah heard the voice of God.

"Before you knew me, I knew you," God said. "Even before you were born, I set you apart. I appointed you a prophet to the nations," Wow! Jeremiah's life did not begin with Jeremiah. It began with God. Jeremiah's *"before"* was not just the Jewish world that existed when he was conceived in his mother's womb. His *"before"* began in the mind of God. And, while still only in the mind of God, Jeremiah received an appointment. The word translated as "appointed" is the Hebrew word *nathan*, which literally means "gave." God is an awesome, lavish, hilarious giver. Before Jeremiah was even conceived, God gave him away. Not just to the Jews. God gave him to the "nations."

Eugene Peterson says, "This is God's way. He did it with his own son. He gave him away. He gave him to the nations. He did not keep him on display. He did not preserve him in a museum. He did not show him off as a trophy." God loved in such a way that He gave His son to the world.

Is it too much to think that God does the same thing with each of His disciples? That is, God knows the exact world into which we will be born, and He gives each of us the necessities to meet the needs of that particular world. For example, would it be presumptuous of me to think that God has prepared me through many years of study to give me at this exact moment to you in these words that you are reading? I have been readied by years of study, not just in educational institutions, but in the school of hard knocks to write these words for you to read at this moment. He blessed me with an early interest in the Bible and in Him, and He has given me opportunity after opportunity to learn. And He did it in order for me to give these words to you today. Could it be that my entire life of preparation is, at this moment, a gift of what God put in me for you?

Is it possible to live life like that? If so, the question is, "To whom has God given you?" What has He put in you that others need? How has He prepared you to meet the needs of the people you bump into in your daily life? Jesus teaches that our life is for others. He taught that, and He lived that. Is it sensible, rational, and joyful to live life from that perspective?

Of course, our culture stands these ideas on their head. The pervasive philosophy of today is "I have the right to live life to meet my needs." Jesus recognized that each of us has physical and emotional needs, and we must make sure those are met. He recognized when He was thirsty and asked directly for water. He knew when He was tired and needed sleep, and He found rest. But He did not live all of His life from the perspective that He was to grab for all the gusto He could get. For Him, others were never merely a means to an end.

God has placed each of us among people who need the rich resources that God has implanted in us. Our life experience is unique. But our life experiences neatly fit the needs of those with whom we interact. God has arranged life that way. No one is unnecessary. We are all needed because we all have areas of influence that offer opportunities to help. Such small things as a smile, an encouraging word, or a hug can be an uplifting inspiration to another.

I am constantly heartened by the story of Esther in the Old Testament. Esther was a beautiful young Jewish woman who had been orphaned as a child and raised by Mordecai, her cousin. She rose to be the queen of Persia. When her husband, King Xerxes, decreed that all Jews be put to death, Mordecai prevailed upon her to beg the king to withdraw his ruling. To do so was a high-stakes effort on her part because it would reveal her as a Jew. Mordecai framed his request with these renowned words, "Who knows but that you came to the kingdom for such a time as this" (Esther 4:14). Her efforts proved a success, and the Persian Jews were saved.

Few of us are called to such an explicitly life and death situation as Queen Esther. But never denigrate the far-reaching impact we can have on the life of another. Who knows the depth at which God is working in the life of a family member, friend, fellow worker, or casual acquaintance with whom we interact? Paul reminds us in Ephesians 1:11 (NLT) that "we have received an inheritance from God, for he chose us in advance, and he makes everything work out according to his plan."

Jeremiah could have remained in Anathoth and served as a dignified priest, following in his father's footsteps. No one would blame him for doing so. But he responded to God's plan. For forty years, he ministered in Jerusalem. Daily, he preached in the streets and was rejected, rebuffed, spit upon, and imprisoned. He preached to Jerusalem, and he preached to the world. He did that because God "gave him to the nations." And now, centuries later, what he preached still impacts us today. So, the question remains, "To whom has God given you?"

What Are We Doing to Our Children?

I write today with a heavy heart. I am sad and I am angry at the same time. These two powerful emotions are all balled up inside me. Why? Because of the question that stands as the title of this essay. No person with normal human compassion who gets even a glimpse at what modern America is doing in mass to her children could fail to share these deep feelings with me. Chimpanzees, we are told, sometimes eat their own offspring. Well, the sad truth is that humans are capable of doing the same thing!

It turns out that we live in a time when the "home of the brave and the land of the free" is not a good place for children. Liberty is defined as freedom from restraint of any kind, especially in the sexual area. Each person, according to the dominant philosophy of our time, gets to define what is right for himself. No one may stand in judgment of another person's code of ethics. Each one decides what is the meaning of life and how one is to go about living it. One writer described this view of life as the "tyranny of relativity."

Ours is a culture that stresses freedom from restraint, offers a life without rules and boundaries, and encourages each person to discover truth for oneself. That may look like a utopia from the perspective of an adult. But from the vantage point of a child, it is a world of confusion, uncertainty, and frustration. It is as if we send a child into a game that has no name, no rules, and no boundaries. Such a game makes no sense, has no score, and no purpose. One does not know which way to run with the ball or what to do with it when you get there. You don't know what is expected and, therefore, have no way of knowing how well you're doing. Even a child knows that if everyone wins, no one wins!

This world without guidelines has cratered the mental health of children in the last few years. Growth in mental health rates for persons aged 10–14 grew at an alarming rate. Fifteen percent of persons aged 5–17 received treatment for a mental disorder in 2021. That number does not include those who needed help and did not receive it during that time frame. Anxiety and depression rates grew by 21 percent from 2016 to 2019 among the young. For children aged 10–14, suicide rates tripled from 2017 to 2018. Workers in the mental health field report the alarming fact that 50 percent of chronic mental health disorders start before age fourteen.[15]

Death rates among American children are on the rise. Of course, they are killed in accidents just as adults are. But they are killing themselves with drug overdose and suicide in increasing numbers. In 2020, mortality rates increased for persons aged 1 to 19 by 10.7 percent and increased by another 8.3 percent in 2021 (the highest two-year rate of increase in the fifty years of keeping track). Many causes are listed for the sudden upward swing. But among them must be that in the last few decades, there has been an unceasing eroding of institutions given the task of teaching the young the values and norms of our culture.

---

[15] See as an example, Reno, RR, "Sacrificing the Young," First Things, August/September 2023. pp 65–66. See also, "No Place for Young Children" Washington Examiner, July 25, 2023, p2 and Eberstadt, Mary, Adam and Eve After the Pill, Revisited, Ignatius Press: San Francisco, pp 13–14, 20, 108–122.

To accommodate a tiny minority of sexually marginalized individuals in the name of "inclusion," we have thrown out any understanding of sexually appropriate behaviors. The single remaining exception to this statement is pedophilia. But the betting money is that even that deviant behavior will soon become acceptable in our "freedom-loving" society. The argument is that we will all be better off when any idea of "normal" is gone from sexuality.

What effect does this philosophy have on a child? It doesn't take a degree in child psychology to recognize that children suffer stress when stability and structure go missing in their lives. They need rules and boundaries that cause life to make sense. They need pathways to follow so that they have a sense of purpose in their life (actually, that fact is true for all of us, no matter the age). The LGBT activists seek to build a world in which the stability and structure of social expectations are gone. They want all of us to believe and act as if truth is something that each person builds out of our own desires and needs. That does not work well for adults. But it makes a child go crazy.

What does it do to children to be instructed that masculinity and femininity are social constructs that one may choose as one wishes? What happens when restrooms and locker rooms, once zones of safety and privacy, are now areas that require vigilance and care? Pronouns and other words require careful attention and risk offense? Drag queens visit libraries and read books to preschoolers, and the Los Angeles Dodgers present "The Sisters of Perpetual Indulgence" with a community award on "LGBTQ Night"? How do children interpret these and other signals from a deviant subculture? And what impact do these things have on the psyche of the developing child?

Jesus once spoke of the value of a child. Sitting down, He took a child into His lap. Wrapping His arms around the tiny body of the child and looking directly into the faces of the crowd, He said, "Whoever receives one such child in my name, receives me. And I say to you, whoever offends one of these little ones, it would be better that a millstone was hanged about his neck and he be thrown into the depth of the sea" (Matthew 18:5–6, ESV).

There is an ancient Jewish proverb that Jesus surely had in mind, which says, "Whoever saves a child, saves a world." The value of a child, besides being a human created in the image of God, always lies in the possibilities that are locked up inside. To place a child in a situation where that potential is stifled and stunted is to "offend" the child, and Jesus uses the harshest possible statements to declare how serious that offense is. It would be better that the offender be dumped into the Mediterranean Sea with a huge millstone tied about his neck.

Wiliam Barclay once wrote, "No Christian can be satisfied to live complacently and lethargically in a civilization where there are conditions of living, [...] and life in general where a young person has no chance of escaping the seduction of sin." Unfortunately, we live in such a civilization. However, Jesus concluded His comments on the value of a child by noting that each child has an angel that always beholds the Father's face. Perhaps Michael is fighting even now for the children.

Maybe the pendulum has begun to swing back. Woke culture standing on the philosophy of a deviant sexual subculture has seen its day, and parents, pastors, a few educators, one or two in the media, and other vigilant persons are beginning to wake up and push back. Let us pray they may be heard for the sake of the children and our country.

Do You Wait Well?

"Jesus loved Martha and her sister and Lazarus. Yet when he heard that Lazarus was sick, he stayed where he was for two more days" (John 11:5–6, ISV).

Sometimes, we are so familiar with Bible stories that we fail to see the unexpected. Jesus often did things that were out of the ordinary. Common sense would expect a certain behavior from Him, yet He does the very opposite. And because we have heard the story a hundred times, we miss the surprise which He intended for us to see. Such is never more true than His totally unanticipated response to the message He got, which is described in the verses quoted above.

Jesus and His disciples were about a day's journey north of Bethany, the home village of Lazarus and his sisters, when a messenger brought Him the news that Lazarus was very sick. Jesus was a frequent visitor to their home and was clearly a close friend to them and loved them. Yet, when told that Lazarus was sick, rather than rush to his side, He remained where He was for two days. There is no implication that He was too busy to drop everything and go to His friend's sick bed. He simply stayed where He was for two days.

Jesus' deliberate delay put the sisters and other concerned persons through a painful waiting period. They constantly watched the road north in hopes of seeing His approach. They prayed for His appearance with worried brows and feverish hands. Then their brother died, and they buried Him. Still, Jesus did not appear. They set about the grieving period, all the while still watching for Jesus to come to them.

Have you ever had a similar experience? There is something of substance that you deeply desire. You pray about your desire and earnestly beseech God to grant your petition. You ask friends to join you in prayer for your entreaty. Nothing happens. God seems to be absent, busy elsewhere. There is no response one way or the other. My mother had a wise question taped to her refrigerator door: "When God seems away, who moved?" Nonetheless, you cannot but ask, "Why?" You find no satisfaction in the answers you give yourself. All you can do is wait. And waiting is always hard!

Waiting is seen in our over-busy culture as passively biding our time for some anticipated event to occur. We view it negatively as a waste and to be avoided, if at all possible. In God's economy, however, waiting is a powerful positive force for good in the believer's life. The great British pastor of the 1800s, Charles Haddon Spurgeon, once wrote, "The waiting itself is beneficial to us: it tries faith, exercises patience, trains submission, and endears the blessing when it comes."

Did you know that the word "passive" comes from a Latin root which means "to endure"? Enduring is not a characteristic of the weak. It demands strength. One "holds on" or "sticks with it." That kind of waiting can be a test of character and perseverance. It can teach us patience, resilience, and determination. It is an opportunity for spiritual growth and self-discovery.

In my own experience, waiting prayerfully on God has taught me more than anything how much I need God. I may think that God is absent, but the truth is that God is never gone. He is always closer to me than my breath. I can, however, see myself alone and God somewhere off busy with "important things." (I may get angry at God for this, or I may throw a pity party for myself. But I never blame myself.) But when I think God is absent and I see myself alone, I realize how helpless I am without God. These times teach me how much I need Him. I realize that He created me for a loving relationship with Him, and I am less than myself when I have lost contact with Him.

Mandy Hale, a contemporary writer of humorous books for women, writes, "What we are waiting for is not as important as what happens to us while we are waiting." This process in which God is carefully building our character, our spirituality, and our trust in Him is far more important than the thing we are waiting for. This truth is made abundantly clear in the life of Jesus. Hebrews 5:7–8 (ESV) tells us that Jesus lifted up His voice in prayer with "loud cries and tears" and that He "learned obedience through what he suffered."

Think about the hands of Jesus. With those hands, He reached out to touch and heal blind persons, paralyzed persons, dead and sick persons. They were loving hands that once had shaped wood and masonry to build homes and furniture for people. They fed hungry crowds and held scrolls that contained the Word of God. With those hands, He healed lepers and motioned for individuals to come and follow Him. Now, at Calvary, those hands were pierced by steel and penned to a cross. He could do nothing. His hands were still, waiting. Never was God closer to Him than in that waiting time. History's most momentous event occurred during that stillness. Nothing in all of time and space can begin to compare with what He accomplished in that time when His hands waited.

The word "human" comes from the Latin *humus*. Did you know that "humus" means "fertile ground"? Thus, to call ourselves human beings means that we are like the earth. We get the word "humility" from that same root. To be humble is not, as many suppose, to try to convince others that we see ourselves as valueless. It is to be like the earth, like fertile soil that always waits, ready to be tilled, planted, and bear fruit. As a farmer, I love this picture of the soil ready to do what it was created to do. That is what it means to be a human being. We wait patiently, with eager anticipation for God's tilling and planting, for slow growth and maturing for the crop God will harvest. When we see our life and the waiting we are called to do, from that perspective, waiting loses all its unpleasant qualities.

Jesus appeared in Bethany in His time because He sought to give Mary, Martha, and Lazarus a greater blessing than they could imagine. His plan required His timing for its full effect. They had to wait, and during that waiting time, God was at work in their life in the same way He was after Jesus showed up. We do not always see what God is up to. We can't possibly know what good He has in mind. But we can "wait well" in trust to see what good He is producing in our lives.

In Part

"Now we know in part, but then..." (1 Corinthians 13:12).

Years ago, a salesman was making the rounds of a rural community in Alabama seeking to sell subscriptions to *Progressive Farmer* magazine. He stopped at a farmhouse where an elderly farmer was sitting in a rocker on the front porch. They chatted for a few minutes about the weather, and then the salesman turned to his sales pitch. He went over the advantages to the farmer of the monthly magazine containing news articles of the latest research. He pointed out the beautiful pictures and short inserts with timely reminders of seasonal interests and market changes. "*Progressive Farmer* will make you a better farmer!" he exclaimed, extending a subscription application toward the farmer. "I don't need that," the farmer explained, shaking his head. "I ain't farmin' now as good as I know how."

This little joke, which I heard first when I was a young man, raises a significant issue that each person who takes Jesus seriously must address. The farmer admits that he knows things about farming, which he fails to put into practice. He also admits that he does not wish to continue learning about farming and that he is satisfied with his present level of farming, haphazard though it might be. Here is the question each of us must answer: Am I like that farmer in my faith? Am I satisfied with what I now "know"?

Let us begin with the admission that, as Paul wrote in 1 Corinthians 13:12, "In this life, we know only in part." Paul knows that our searching and enquiring mind has available in Jesus the perfect revelation of God and the perfect standard of living and relating to our fellowman. Yet, though Jesus is the exact image of God in the flesh, we can grasp only a part. The finite cannot fully comprehend the infinite. Our knowledge, he notes in verse 11, is like that of a child when we are dealing with eternal things. We see only partial reflections of God "Through a mirror darkly." Mirrors in Paul's day were made of highly shined metal, and no matter how polished they were, they produced only indistinct reflections. Our study always leaves us with mysteries because our brains are not capable of thought on God's level.

Moses once asked to see God (Exodus 33:18–23). God agreed to allow "all His goodness" to pass by in front of Moses. "But," God said, "You cannot see my face, because no one can see my face and live." God passed by, and Moses was privileged to see God's back. What Moses saw was less than the full revelation of God. Once again, we are left with a mystery for which there is no answer. Something real happened that day, but we are not altogether sure what exactly it was.

Our faith is not irrational. It makes sense. It describes reality and offers a path that leads to joy, peace, meaning, and purpose. When Jesus promised "eternal life" to those who commit their life to Him, He was not offering everlasting life on a cloud playing a harp. He was promising that the things that matter—things like love, intimacy, caring, understanding, satisfaction, encouragement, and inspiration—these things and more are the qualities of heaven. And, most importantly, believers receive a foretaste of these things *in this life!* We enter "eternal life" the moment we believe in Him.

Jesus spoke often of "knowing Him." Once, He said, "You shall know the truth, and the truth will set you free" (John 8:32). These are lofty words and are often quoted, even in secular settings. Scientists and other educators who are not believers borrow these words from Jesus and have no idea what He meant when He said them or how they apply to the lives of believers today.

The verse immediately before this statement sets the scene. It begins, "So Jesus said to the Jews who had come to believe in him...." Jesus was in Jerusalem and was embroiled in a running conflict with the Pharisees and chief priests. The Jewish leadership was anxious because His miracles and teachings were drawing great crowds, and many people were becoming His followers. In the midst of this increasing tension, He addressed His recent converts, "If you hold to my teaching, you are really my disciples. Then you will know the truth and the truth will set you free" (John 8:31–32).

It would be difficult to find words that give a more complete description of discipleship. "Holding to His teaching" means to be a learner. Jesus is our rabbi (teacher), and we are life-long learners (students). This learning is more than mental assent to philosophical or historical facts. It is more than the acquisition of a skill, like riding a bicycle or driving a car. Rather, it is more like coming to know a person in friendship and intimacy. For example, in a meaningful marriage, a man and woman continually grow in their knowledge, care, and fellowship throughout their years together. It is learning that is never complete.

Further, discipleship results in obedience. Our relationship with Jesus, unlike a friendship or marriage, is not the uniting of two equals. He is the Lord, and we are His servants. He loves us with unconditional love; it is true. But "holding to His teachings" means that we obey His directions and do what He says (Luke 6:46).

In His teaching, we find the mind of God. That statement is explosive. The teachings of Jesus conveyed in the pages of the New Testament can be disturbing, even dangerous, in the extent to which they can change our lives. Paul describes how radical that change can be in Ephesians 5:8. He says that once we were "darkness," but now we are "light." That entire chapter lists the sweeping changes that Jesus' teaching can bring into our lives.

Discipleship brings "knowledge of the truth that sets us free." His truth shows us the real values in life. Everyone asks, either consciously or unconsciously, "To what shall I give my life?" He answers that question, and finding His answer to that question sets us free to live the life He promised. In that life is the only place where we can find genuine freedom.

Let us remember that we always "know in part." Learning Jesus is our privilege and joy throughout life. It is a "study" that never ends. Are you a "farmer" who wants to improve and never stop learning?

Little Things

"You have been faithful over little things..." (Matthew 25:21).

I love the story of Martin of Tours. Born in 316 in what is now Hungary, he became a Christian at age ten and joined the military when he was fifteen. He quickly became a leader of men and rose swiftly through the ranks. After an especially fierce battle, he approached the gates of Amiens in northern France with a group of his men. He was met there by a beggar, nearly frozen in the wintery cold. Martin had no money to give him, but, stepping down from his horse, he tore his battle-scarred military coat in two and gave half to the beggar.

That night, Martin dreamed that he was in heaven, where he saw Jesus wearing half a ragged military coat. As Martin watched, an angel asked Jesus, "Where did you get that old piece of coat?" Jesus responded, "My servant Martin gave it to me when I was freezing in the winter's cold." Soon, Martin left the military and later became the pastor of the church at Tours, also in northern France, where he served till his death in 397.

I love this story because it communicates two great truths. First, little things count greatly in God's kingdom. God does not overlook the giving of half a ragged coat. Secondly, little things that we do can change the direction of our lives and impact us more than those who receive our gifts. The beggar was warmed for a few nights with that coat, but the direction of Martin's life was changed. Martin was never the same after that night.

The Bible is full of praise for little things. For example, James 3:4 reminds us that great ships are guided by small rudders. In Matthew 13:31, Jesus praised faith that is small, like a mustard seed. Zechariah 4:10 (NLT) admonishes us, "Do not despise these small beginnings. For the Lord rejoices to see the work begin." In Luke 21:2, Jesus praised the widow who dropped two pennies into the collection plate. First Samuel 17:40 gives us an interesting detail about when David went out to meet Goliath: "He stooped to collect from the river bed five smooth stones." In 1 Corinthians 1:27, Paul states, "God has chosen the foolish and weak things to confound the wise of the world." Later, in 2 Corinthians 12:10, Paul announces, "I delight in weakness... for when I am weak, then I am strong." And when Jesus faced feeding a crowd of 5,000, one of the disciples said, "There is a lad here with five barley loaves and two fish. But what are they among so many?" (John 6:9). We know the answer to that question.

The scripture quoted at the head of this essay comes from a parable that Jesus told during the last week of His physical life on earth (Matthew 25:14–30). It is a story of a rich man leaving for a journey who divides some of his wealth among three of his servants. They were to invest his money while he was gone and return it with its gain when he returned. Two were diligent, and the man praised them for their good work, saying, "You have been faithful with little things, and I will reward you by placing you over great things" (Matthew 25:21). The third, fearing the wrath of the rich man, failed and received no such reward. In fact, what he had was taken from him and given to the other two.

This is, like all of Jesus' stories, a profound tale with many applications to our lives. What interests me at this point is what Jesus said after He told this story. Matthew 25:31–46 follows directly on the heels of the story of the three servants. His intent is to answer the question, "What are the little things over which His followers are to be faithful?" Without missing a beat, Jesus moves smoothly into a story about judgment. He will separate the "sheep from the goats" (Matthew 25:32), He says, according to what they have done with little things. Jesus said, "I am going to say to some, 'You gave me food when I was hungry, you gave me water when I was thirsty, you welcomed me when I was isolated, you gave me clothes when I had none, you looked after me when I was sick, and when I was in prison, you visited me'" (Matthew 25:35–36).

Jesus by no means intends to say that the great things done through the centuries—great books written, great sermons preached, great sums given, great movements which brought many to the feet of Jesus, great hymns written—are of no value. We may all thank God for men and women through the ages who have spent their lives making certain that the message of the Gospel was not lost to history. We needed the Billy Grahams of every century. What He is saying is that the rest of us, common, everyday people with our little things, are not unimportant in God's eyes. Jesus said that even a cup of cold water given because one is a disciple will not be forgotten (Matthew 10:42).

John D. Rockefeller said that "the secret of success is to do common things uncommonly well." Mother Teresa reminds us to do little things with great love. Humphry Davy, a British inventor and chemist in the early 1800s, wrote, "Life is made up, not of grand sacrifices or duties, but of little things in which smiles and kindness, and small obligations given habitually are what preserve the heart and secure comfort." And Benjamin Franklin noted, "Little strokes fell great oaks."

We are talking here about tiny, everyday things that we can do for our fellow humans because we are followers of Jesus. A smile, a pat on the back, a sincere compliment, a word of encouragement, stopping to listen, a thank you, a wink, a greeting, a wave of the hand, or a nod of the head. Maya Angelou, an amazing woman of poetry, once said, "People do not remember what you say. They do not remember what you do. But they will never forget how you make them feel." She is right in the overall sentiment of this statement. What people remember about us, more than our words and acts, is how we make them feel about themselves and their place in the world. In fact, our words and acts reveal our attitudes and are the avenue by which we contribute to how others feel.

Let us remember that our own character emerges from the configuration of all the little things we are too busy to do but do anyway. We engage what Abraham Lincoln called "our better angels" by the little things we do for others. Besides, it makes me happy to do little things for those with whom I interact in a normal day's activities. Who knows, my "little" may be a "big" to them. Also, I try to keep in mind that Jesus said that when I do little things for them, I "do it for Him." That means my kindness to a fellow traveler along life's path is a gift I give to Him that I want to do.

The Judas Heart

"Happy are those whose hearts are pure. They will see God!" (Matthew 5:8, author's translation).

It was the Tuesday evening of the last week of Jesus' life. Jerusalem was filled to overflowing with visitors from all over the world, having come to celebrate Passover. He was there not to celebrate Passover but to be Passover. He and several of His followers were in the home of Simon the Leper, enjoying a sumptuous meal with some of the minor elite of the city. Simon was evidently a well-known victim of leprosy whom Jesus had healed (he might even be the only one of the ten lepers who returned to thank Jesus). The banquet was given by Simon in Jesus' honor. No one but Jesus knew what was to come on Friday.

As they reclined to eat the evening meal, Mary, the sister of Martha and Lazarus, came and knelt beside Jesus. She carried a small vial of nard, an expensive perfume imported from India. She broke the alabaster container and poured the contents on the head and feet of Jesus. Tears fell on His feet, and she carefully dried them with her hair.

At once, loud whispers arose from the crowd, with the voice of Judas most prominent. The vial of perfume would have cost the equal of a year's wages. "Why this blasphemous waste?" they asked. "This perfume could have been sold and the money given to the poor."

Jesus, however, took exception to their objection. "Leave her alone," He said. "Her act is a lovely thing. She has anointed me for burial." He knew that those convicted of a crime were not anointed for burial. In fact, most were not buried at all. Taken from the cross, they were thrown into a huge ditch near Golgotha to rot and become food for the buzzards. Other than Mary's act, Jesus' body was never anointed.

Mary's act was motivated by gratitude. She loved Jesus, and He had been an important of her life. Her desire was to show, not just with words but with action, how deeply grateful she was. She also knew that He loved her. For Mary, no gift was too expensive to show how deeply she loved Him.

The story takes a sudden turn at this point. With no warning and without a single goodbye or thank you, Judas got up and left the banquet. He knew exactly where he was going and what he would do. In a matter of minutes, he was with the chief priests, making arrangements to betray Jesus. These deeply religious leaders were both surprised and delighted with his offer and willingly entered into haggling with him about how much they would pay for his help in finding and arresting Jesus. They finally arrived at an acceptable price: thirty pieces of silver, a half year's daily wage.

Scripture scholars have offered a number of interpretations of Judas's motivation. Time and space do not allow for an examination of them. Suffice it to say Mary and Judas had arrived at the same conclusion. They both saw that Jesus was on a collision course with the authorities and that they were going to kill Him. For Judas, that thought brought only bitter disappointment. After all, he had sunk three years into following Jesus all over the Holy Land. He had been committed to the idea that, as the Messiah, Jesus would lead an insurrection against the Romans and drive them into the sea. No way that was going to happen. The religious leaders and the Romans were going to destroy Him rather than the other way around.

His decision to betray Jesus rested upon his desire to cut his losses. *There is no future here*, he realized, so he was getting out. Rather than trusting Jesus, the only thing Jesus required, he trusted himself. Who better than he could direct his life? We know, of course, that as a result of his act, he killed himself, and his body was thrown into a ditch for the buzzards' next meal.

Two guests shared this meal with Jesus, and each had their own private thoughts and motivations. One heart was filled with sadness, joy, love, and gratitude. That heart sought to demonstrate her adoration and praise in an unselfish spirit of giving. The other heart was filled with self-centered calculations and anger. One heart asked, *How can I show Him how much I love Him?* The other heart was bitter with disappointment. This heart said, *Jesus is not doing what I want Him to do. How can I salvage for myself something out of this failure?* One heart was about to encounter a resurrected savior, and the other was headed for an unmarked grave.

We can still see these two attitudes toward Jesus among His followers today. In fact, I suspect these two are, at varying degrees of intensity, the only options open to His followers. Either you give Him your life in gratitude and love, or you insist on doing things your own way. You see, Judas's sin was not that he betrayed Jesus. His betrayal was an outward act that was the *outcome of his sin.* His sin was *internal.* In his heart, he trusted Judas, not Jesus. He would act on his own schemes to take care of himself. His thinking was, *I know what is good for me, and I am going to follow my will!*

That inward willfulness was the sin of Adam and Eve and is the space where all disobedient acts originate. And on Sunday mornings, our pews are often occupied by people who have that exact attitude. (I must confess that the pew where I sit is too often where this attitude can be found.) The Judas heart did not die with Judas.

We do not know what went on in Judas from the time he kissed Jesus to identify him to the arresting soldiers and the moment he hung himself. And we do not know what happened to him the moment after he died. We do know Jesus' attitude toward him as he clung to the cross. He prayed, "Father, forgive them. They do not know what they are doing." We can, however, imagine what Judas was feeling during that time. Without a doubt, he was overwhelmed with guilt and sadness, for which the end of his life seemed the only relief. How sad.

Mary, on the other hand, while understandably saddened at the cruelty and rejection to which Jesus had been subjected, was overwhelmed with joy at His resurrection. Her heart was blessed, and, as Jesus promised, she saw God. My prayer is, "God, give me a heart like Mary." Is that your prayer?

• CHAPTER 6 •

God's Help Along the Way

The most powerful prayer you can pray is, "Lord Jesus, I don't know what to do. Help me." So often, we come to God with a list of problems and an equal list of our suggested solutions for each one. Our prayer is often no more than a frenzied effort to get God to do what we wish. We must remember that there is nothing wrong with presenting our petitions, our desires, and our deepest wants to our Father in heaven. God has invited us to do so in many places in the Bible. But never let yourself forget that He, and He alone, is our "ever present help in time of trouble" (Psalm 46:1, BSB). He, not what He does, is the solution to our problems. That is the promise of Isaiah 41:10: "So do not fear, for I am with you; do not be dismayed, for I and your God. I will strengthen you and help you; I will uphold you with my righteous right hand."

Just When We Need Him Most

Martin Luther King Jr.'s favorite song was written by a man named Thomas Dorsey. Dorsey, the son of a Georgia farmer and Baptist minister, wrote over 3,000 published songs. King's favorite was Dorsey's song, "Precious Lord, Take My Hand." To further his musical career, Dorsey had moved from Atlanta to Chicago, where he wrote and recorded mostly blues songs. His first recorded song was entitled, "If You Don't Believe I'm Leaving, You Can Count the Days I'm Gone," Ultimately, he turned to sacred music and became the choral director of the huge Pilgrim Baptist Church in Chicago.

Dorsey had traveled from his home in Chicago to St. Louis for a "singing school" at a local Baptist church in August 1932. While there, he received word that his wife, Nettie, had died in childbirth along with their baby. Overwhelmed with grief, Dorsey sat down at a piano and sang the words, "Precious Lord, take my hand, lead me on, let me stand. I am tired, I am weak, I am worn. Through the storm, through the night, lead me on to the light. Take my hand, precious Lord, lead me home."

The message of the song touched the heart of King, who carried a great burden and daily faced struggles and danger beyond the ability of a normal man. He often asked Mahalia Jackson to sing Dorsey's song at his meetings and public occasions. It was his request that she sing the song at his funeral, and it was the only hymn sung at his graveside.

I suppose there are times when we all go through the valley of greatest need. Life is hard, and each of us, in our own way, is called on to face the darkness of uncertainty and doubt when we need the precious Lord to take our hand and lead us home to the light. I often think of how much our life is exactly like the experiences described in the life of Jesus with His disciples. These events in the New Testament are recorded to help us see ourselves and our situation and to find guidance and assurance when we need it.

For example, consider the story of the disciples crossing a stormy sea at night (Matthew 14:22–46, recorded also in Mark and John). This story came immediately after Jesus had fed the 5,000 with the lunch of a lad. He sent (the Greek says that He "compelled") the disciples to go on ahead of Him across the Sea of Galilee while He stayed behind to disperse the crowd. After dismissing them, He went up into the mountains to pray. Night fell before He finished His praying. By this time, the boat carrying the disciples was far out into the trip across the sea.

The Sea of Galilee is located such that it frequently erupts with furious wind and rain storms. The desert 200 to 400 miles to the east produces high winds that are hot and dry. They come from the southeast, sweeping into the mountain range, cupping the area that is the north side of modern-day Iraq. This mountain range is like the top half of a circle, which catches the winds, sends them around the circle, and reverses their direction toward the south. These severe winds head directly over the Sea of Galilee, and when their hot and dry constituency meets the moist air rising from the Sea of Galilee, suddenly furious, devastating storms erupt. The boat filled with the disciples ran into such a storm.

It was not until the fourth watch of the night (3:00 to 6:00 a.m.) that Jesus went out to them (Matthew 4:25). We must not miss the significance of the timing here. It is as if Jesus deliberately allowed them time to fight with the storm. Our struggle does at least two things for us. First, it increases the strength of our faith. We learn that in the hour of our greatest need, Jesus comes to us. God's timing is always designed to increase our trust, and our faith in Him is never misplaced. Second, our fight forces us to the realization of how much we need Him. Our struggle, so often futile against the wind and rain, teaches us how great our helplessness is without Him.

Jesus comes to them in the midst of the storm, walking on the water (Matthew 14:25). When the disciples saw this ghostly-looking creature floating as if on air, they were terrified. Isn't it strange that the very thing that was to resolve their problem was something that made them afraid? There is a principle here that we cannot miss. When we try to resolve our problem without God, we most often want a solution that costs us little or nothing and is fast and easy. Not so with God. He often asks us to face our fears, change some aspects of ourselves, and do things that are generous, forgiving, and self-sacrificing. He urges us, in the words of Paul, "Do not be conformed to this world, but be transformed..." (Romans 12:2, ESV). If you wish to know what He asks of us, read chapters 5–7 of Matthew. These chapters answer the question, "How, then, shall we live?"

So, in their hour of need, Jesus came to them. He was aware of their fear, and He calmed them. He called on them first to have courage. Courage is the virtue that allows us to go forward even when we are afraid. *Feel the Fear and Do It Anyway!* by Susan Jeffers is the title of the best book I know on courage and fear. That is what Jesus asks for. You are in a storm that looks like it will take your life. God bursts into the scene, which only heightens your fear.

"Take courage" is Jesus' admonition to us when we are afraid. Do it anyway. We know the truth of what Jesus is saying. The only way to overcome stage fright is to get on the stage. One way to overcome the fear of flying is to get on airplanes. Any person who has participated successfully in a twelve-step program knows that victory over any addiction comes only when we face the very thing that we fear the most. It is the way God created reality.

"It is I," Jesus identifies Himself. Does that soothe your fear when you realize that Jesus is in the storm with you? It is a promise He makes to us. In the upper room the night before His crucifixion, Jesus wanted to prepare His followers for the uncertainty and doubt they would feel the next day. He wanted to assure them that not even death could separate them from His love and presence. So, He said, among many other assurances, "I will not leave you orphans. I will come to you…. On that day, you will realize that I am in my father, and you are in me and I am in you" (John 14:18; 14:20).

In life, the storms are tough. We often get up against it. Life is a fight, and sometimes our strength runs short. It is a time like that when our faith says that we are not alone. He comes when we need Him most, and He stills the storm outside, or He stills the storm inside. He says, "Take courage. It is I."

Dancing on the Edge of a Volcano

An article in *The Washington Examiner*, a conservative and secular news magazine, by Ian Corbin caught my attention last week. It was entitled "Dancing on the Edge of a Volcano." Corbin asked an interesting question about the death of George Floyd, a black man, at the hands of Derek Chauvin, a white Minneapolis police officer. This event set off massive waves of protests, riots, killing, and looting around the country. Corbin asks, why now? Since 2013, close to 1,000 people, roughly one-third of them black, have been killed by police officers. Why has this one thrown our country into such turmoil, murder, and destruction? No other death has created anything like this in our nation and around the world.

Briefly put, Corbin's answer is that for the last three hundred years, the West has been caught in social forces that have separated us from the stability of family, faith, and community. Modern life—big cities, crowded freeways, impersonal neighborhoods, cutthroat competition, untrustworthy government, disrupted families, empty and meaningless churches—has brought about a transition to the kind of world for which human beings have been biologically, psychologically, and spiritually unprepared.[16]

We have experienced traumatic losses in this transition. We are separated from God, from a sense of community, a nearness and involvement with nature, and a certainty of the meaning and purpose of life. The promises of this glimmering new world were unimaginable freedom and prosperity. It has failed to deliver on its promises, and the bread and circuses it provided have vanished or grown stale. Underneath this world of alienated and lost people is a volcano awaiting eruption. What we have seen of the recent rage and hatred is one small demonstration of human dissatisfaction with the modern world we now inhabit.

Fifty years ago, anthropologist Desmond Morris published a book entitled *The Human Zoo*. In it, he likened the effects of

---

16 Corbin, I. M. (2020) Dancing on the Edge of a Volcano, Washington Examiner. Available at: https://www.washingtonexaminer.com/opinion/dancing-on-the-edge-of-a-volcano (Accessed: 13 November 2023).

"civilized living" on human beings to the effect the zoo has on animals. We are made to live in touch with nature and live in close, small communities and extended families. However, we have reconstructed our environment to live today in a huge, impersonal, inhumane collection of concrete called cities. Deeply disturbing psychological, physical, social, and spiritual results are the result. We pay the piper for the music we request.

More recently (2022), biologists Heather Heying and Bret Weinstein made basically the same argument in their book, *A Hunter-Gatherer's Guide to the 21st Century*. Their thesis is seen in the title of the book. Psychologically, physically, emotionally, socially, and (I would add) spiritually, we are hunters and gatherers trying to fit ourselves into the 21st century way of life. They point out in many ways in their well-researched book that human beings are totally out of place in modern civilization. Their conclusion: "We are headed for collapse. Civilization is becoming incoherent around us."

Corbin's argument, like that of Morris and Heying and Weinstein, is powerful and convincing. Yet, like so many commentators on the world condition, he is excellent at describing the problem but offers little or no solution. I am left wondering, "Is there a path off of this volcano?" The smart guys are almost always silent when this question comes up.

I was sinking into a sense of helplessness when I remembered Abraham Heschel's statement, "God is not nice. God is not an uncle. God is an earthquake." As Christians, we belong to One who disrupts our comfortable life like an earthquake or a volcano. Following Jesus does not mean that we get off the volcano or escape the earthquake. In our day, we are called to live the Gospel in that human zoo. Proof of that point of how God's power shakes things up is the life of Jesus. He disturbed everyone.

Think about Matthew, whose Jewish name was Levi (see Matthew 9:9). Matthew was a young Jew who was following a career that promised him a future. He was already a wealthy man. He lived in a fancy home, wore stylish clothes, and hobnobbed with the Roman power brokers. He had everything, and it did not bother him in the least that everyone hated him. In fact, it pleased him because, as he saw it, they were jealous of his great accomplishments. Then the earthquake hit, and everything came loose.

Jesus passed by. Matthew was in his booth, all safe behind metal bars, with the door locked. No danger could get in to disturb him. The line was long as people waited for him to check his books and state how much in taxes they owed. They insulted him, and some, as they were leaving, spit at him. But he was safe inside. His Roman guard, with a double-edged sword, stood by to protect him from the people's hatred as he made his way home. Nothing could harm him.

Matthew had seen Jesus several times over the last few weeks and was curious about this street preacher. Could He really do what people were claiming? He was startled that Jesus knew his name. "Matthew," Jesus said. Matthew gave a "who, me?" expression on his face. "Yes, you, Matthew, son of Alpheus. Come, follow me."

Matthew gave another look of "You don't mean me, do You?" Jesus said, "Yes, you." Matthew shuffled some papers, closed his books, unlocked the door, and stepped out. He walked away, having no idea where he was going or what he would do when he got there. His parents, his friends, and even the Roman guard tried to talk him out of this foolish decision. But too late. The earthquake had hit, and now everything was different.

That night, Matthew gave a great banquet for Jesus and His disciples. When Matthew began to follow Jesus, he did so openly. No one could doubt that his commitment was real, and no one could doubt that it cost Matthew everything. The advantages his position as tax collector gave were gone, and would never return. His reputation among the Romans was totally destroyed. Among the Jews, the hatred of Matthew because of his connection to the Romans became hatred because he was a believer. The earthquake shook up everything.

We are like Matthew in our own time. But here's the good news: the earthquake is the path that gives us life as we dance on the edge of the volcano. What our time needs from us is to live the life Jesus calls us to live. As believers who live in twenty-first-century America, our commitment to the call of Jesus heals the losses that modernity has stolen from us. We will never return to a hunter-gatherer society, nor would I wish to. Our call today is to live Christ as an earthquake on the edge of the volcano.

How does discipleship help us deal with modernity? According to Corbin and Morris, at the deepest level, the last two centuries have stolen from modern folks a connection with God. Jesus returns us to intimacy with God. Modern man has lost a sense of togetherness and community. Fellowship in the church and intimacy in believing families offer us a sense of community and opportunity for genuine togetherness.

Further, people of the twenty-first century are separated from nature. God gives us ample opportunity to be aware of the beauty and goodness of the earth. Each time we eat, we give thanks to God for the gifts of this wonderful earth. Contemporary humans wander around with no clear understanding of where they are going. Nothing gives greater meaning and purpose in life than becoming a disciple of Jesus.

As I look back over my long life, I am able to thank God for the times He came as an earthquake into my life. I am grateful for the way Jesus has disrupted my life and protected me from the ills of modernity. I say to God, "Keep on shaking things up." Do you say that?

God, What Do We Do When the Brook Runs Dry?

"When you are finished changing, you are finished."
Benjamin Franklin

We know nothing of Elijah's personal life or his upbringing. He just appears as an adult man called by God to be a prophet to the northern kingdom of Israel. The Bible, introducing him, refers to him as a "Tishbite, from the settlers in Gilead." Nothing is known of God's call of him nor God's direction of what he is to do. He simply shows up one day in the presence of the king and confronts him with a straightforward challenge from God. There would be neither rain nor dew until Elijah himself calls on the clouds to gather and the showers to fall.

The king whom he confronts is the infamous Ahab, married to the wicked and equally infamous Jezebel. About Ahab, it is said that he "did more evil in the eyes of the Lord than any of those before him" (1 Kings 16:30). Jezebel, a Phoenician woman of fierce energy and daughter of the Phoenician king, was a devoted worshipper of Baal. The two, as king and queen, ruled Israel for twenty-two years from 874 to 853 BC. They rightly saw Elijah as a powerful enemy whom they plotted to slaughter along with all worshipers of Yahweh in the land. From his first day as a prophet, Elijah's life was in mortal danger.

But God had a plan. He sent His prophet away to the wild and rugged land of Gilead on the east side of the Jordan River. He was to go to "hide" in a deep ravine in which flowed the Kerith brook. Elijah went, and the ravens brought him food, and he drank from the brook. Elijah's physical needs were met by God's providence. (This fact is true for us today. The ravens flew his food in, and ours is delivered by eighteen-wheelers. The method of delivery is different, but the source is the same!) Then, one day, the brook became a trickle, and the next day, there was no water. The drought which consumed the land of Israel had reached Elijah's little hiding place. The Kerith brook, the source of life for the prophet of God, had dried up. Now what?

Heraclitus, an ancient Greek philosopher (born 544 BC) and near contemporary of Elijah, once wrote, "There is nothing permanent but change." His whole philosophy was built around the idea that the only thing that never changes is that everything changes. He also wrote the astounding statement, "No man can step in the same river twice, for it is not the same river, and he is not the same man." We can interpret this statement literally. A man's first step into a river alters the flow of the river slightly, and the pressure of his foot disturbs the river bed. Thus, his second step is into a different river. Further, in the moments between the first step and the second, the man has grown older, and the physical experience of the water against his skin has altered the state of his body. Thus, he is not the same man.

But Heraclitus' wisdom is much deeper than the merely physical level. Life itself is the process of change. It begins with the infant. Safe and secure in her mother's womb, the baby suddenly feels the downward pressure of powerful constrictions that seem to be pushing her away. The pressures mount until the startled infant is forced head-first through a narrow, cave-like passageway. She is ejected from her familiar world into a strange, lighted, noisy new world. All this without considering her wishes. Indeed, she was granted no consultation.

Shakespeare has Guiderius, the star of *Cybeline*, conclude, "Golden lads and girls must / As chimney sweepers, come to dust." Even the beautiful and young must change with time and ultimately return to the earth from which we all have come. Thomas Howard, an orthodox Christian and university professor of English, calls time "the baleful herald of change." Time flies, we know, and brings with it the sure knowledge that nothing in this world lasts. All brooks dry up.

The question then is not "Will change come?" Rather, we must ask, "What does a Christian do when change shows up?" John Maxwell, evangelical pastor and author, says, "Change is inevitable; growth is optional." Change is external and situational. Things change in our outside world. But growth is internal and personal. Change is almost always beyond our control. Things happen to us. Things which, for the most part, we cannot alter or control. How we respond to these changes is within our control and determines the direction of our life. Abraham Lincoln was right when he said, "It is not what happens to you that is important. It is how you respond to what happens to you that makes the difference."

The Bible often refers to growth as "transformation." In those pages, change (that is, outside stuff) can become transformation (inside stuff) as persons grow in their faith and life as Christians. We are told, for example, that we are "being transformed" into a "new image" (2 Corinthians 3:18). Ezekiel and Jeremiah both promise that God's work in us over the years will grow a "new heart and a new spirit" in us.

For me, these are much more than words of "religious jargon" that we say but make no real impact in our lives. These are actual, real-life changes that, when we allow Him, God will grow in us through the vicissitudes of life. He does it for caterpillars. If they enter their cocoon, the little crawling worm-like thing will be transformed in about ten days into a beautiful flying thing called a butterfly. That is never an easy thing for a caterpillar to do. He gives up his known and familiar world and, in a sense, "dies." There is a time period when, in the cocoon, it is neither a caterpillar nor a butterfly. Our transformation can be just as scary and demand just as much trust.

Transformation demands openness. First, an open hand. The extended fingers and upright palm symbolize the release of the old. To get to the far side of a river, one must necessarily leave the near side. We can't hold on to the past. Also, the open hand symbolizes the willingness to accept the new.

Secondly, transformation demands open eyes. Too often, our eyes are stuck on the past, and we miss God's ordinary, everyday miracles today. We have no sense of what God is doing, nor do we see His plan.

And finally, transformation demands an open heart. We invite others in. We look for ways to encourage, inspire, assist, and serve others. We grow when our heart is open to receive God's love in all the ways He chooses to show it. And we show our love for Him by our love of others (Matthew 25:31–46). So, when the brook goes dry, we, like a lowly caterpillar, trust in God and, with anticipation, look for transformation into a beautiful butterfly.

What Is a Blessing?

"Blessed be the God and father of our Lord, Jesus Christ, who has blessed us in the heavenly realms with every spiritual blessing in Christ" (Ephesians 1:3).

It seems to me that words like *blessing, bless, blessedness,* and *blessed* are used today in such a casual and offhanded manner that they have lost all meaning. When someone sneezes, we say, "God bless you." We often hear, even in secular circles, "You have my blessing for that." "Bless your heart" is sometimes used to comfort and reassure a person. "Blessings on you" finds its way into conversations. In religious circles, we often hear the comment, "Bless you." We "ask the blessings" before a meal and sometimes describe a meeting as a "blessed event." We can refer to a situation as a "mixed blessing." "Bless" and its companion words pop up with frequency in our everyday conversation.

I am afraid that we have taken a powerful and authoritative biblical word full of purposeful meaning and made a weak platitude of it. We have little understanding of what we are asking for when we petition God for a blessing for ourselves or others. It is little more today than a generalized wish to signal approval or encouragement. Our emasculated "blessing" has little more meaning than "good luck" or "best wishes." A blessing is often no more than a quick and easy shorthand for a thing conducive to happiness or ordinary well-being.

Actually, the word "bless" turns up on the first page of the Bible. In Genesis 1:22, speaking of living creatures in the waters and birds of the air, and after seeing that they were "good," God "blessed them" and said, "Be fruitful and increase in number." Then, in Genesis 1:28, after creating animals for the dry land and having created Adam and Eve, God "blessed them" and said, "Be fruitful and increase in number, fill the earth, and serve as guardians of it all."

One may readily see that God's blessing in these verses has to do with a great deal more than superficially offering approval and encouragement. God is not saying, "Good luck to you." He is giving power to something or someone to do that for which they are designed or intended to do. All living things are directed by God to multiply and fill the earth. Humans are given a stewardship role, which includes the responsibility of taking care of the earth. God's blessings bestow the capacities necessary to carry out God's intended purpose!

Many scriptures declare that blessing is a two-way street. That is, God blesses us, and we, in turn, bless Him. Psalm 103:1–2 is an example of biblical encouragement for His followers to bless God. "Bless the Lord, O my soul; all my inmost being, bless his holy name. Bless the Lord, O my soul, and forget not all his benefits." This entire psalm is a litany of all the incredible things God has done for us. It is a recognition of God's blessings on us.

Our return blessing of God is our humble gratitude expressed to Him for what He had done for us. Our blessings to Him in the form of praise, worship, dancing, giving, serving, or singing underscore that He is the source of all our blessings, including life itself. Three times a day, all Jews are expected to begin a prayer with the words, "Blessed are you, Lord God, King of the universe." There can be little doubt that Jesus Himself, along with His disciples, prayed these exact words.

Our blessings from God also encourage us to bless others. When God made His covenant with Abram, He promised, "I will make you into a great nation and I will bless you; I will make your name great, and you will be a blessing" (Genesis 12:1–3, BSB). God blesses us so that we may be a blessing. That is, He empowers us to accomplish His purposes for us so that we may help others along the way. To bless others includes praying for God's help in carrying out His will for their life.

When we say to another, "God bless you," we are doing much more than giving a word of encouragement. Our words are a prayer for God's power and guidance in that person's life. And it is a promise that we will continue to pray for that person. When we give food to a hungry man, clean water to a thirsty child, or money to a children's research hospital, we do much more than fill an empty stomach or buy lunch for a medical researcher. We bring the power of God's blessing into a person's life. When I take from my abundance, which came through God's blessing, and give it to another, I am an instrument God uses to deliver His blessing to another.

When the crowd had gathered around Him, according to Matthew 5:1–2, Jesus began His famous Sermon on the Mount. The first word He spoke to them was *makarioi*, which means "blessed." Jesus goes on to give eight statements describing the Christian way of life, and He begins each with that same word. "Supreme happiness" or "a foretaste of the joy of heavenly bliss" is what He is talking about. To those who would entrust their life to God as He is about to describe, God gives the power to find and fulfill the purpose for which God created them.

Makarioi (blessed) is a word frequently used in Greek mythology to describe the gods. Jesus is taking that concept to describe the joy of our faith. It is as if He is saying, "Oh, the blessedness, the supreme bliss, the godlike joy, of following me!"

Cyprus is a particularly beautiful island in the eastern end of the Mediterranean, which was given the nickname *he mikaria* (from *makarioi*), which means "the happy isle." The island was so lovely, its soil so fertile, its climate so perfect, its flowers and fruits and trees so plentiful that there was no need to go beyond her coastline to find anything necessary for an abundant and happy life. God's "blessing" places us on "the happy isle."

Jesus promised "life to the full," "the abundant life" (John 10:10). Paul has the same issue in mind when he says, "God is able to make all grace abound in you, so having all sufficiency in all things at all time, you may abound to all good work" (2 Corinthians 9:8, ESV). God's grace and favor, freely bestowed in God's blessing, in *makarioi*, produce the life about which Jesus and Paul are describing. He created us for that life, He calls us to that life, and He gives us the power to live that kind of life. That is God's blessing offered to us. We bless Him with our praise of gratitude for His grace and favor, and we bless others by aiding their entrance into that kind of life. That is what biblical "blessing" is. And that is why we pray, "Bless us, O God."

All Have Sinned

"All we like sheep have gone astray…" (Isaiah 53:6, ESV).

J. R. Miller was a Presbyterian minister in the late 1800s. He once wrote, "Christ is building his Kingdom with earth's broken things." That sentence caught my attention because it states an unexpected truth. Human beings want the strong, the victorious, the perfect to build our "kingdoms." We shy away from "losers." Who wants to build a business with weak or incompetent individuals? I have personally read the applications of many prospective students seeking entrance to graduate school. I wanted the strongest because, in my opinion, it was the brightest and best who were most likely to succeed.

But not Jesus. He came, He said, "To seek and save the lost" (Luke 19:10). He came to the sick, not the well, because it is they who need a physician (Luke 5:31). He invites "the harassed and helpless" to be His disciples (Matthew 11:28). In His kingdom, it is the poor, the meek, the hungry, the mourning, the merciful, the peacemakers, and the persecuted who are the blessed and who know genuine happiness (Matthew 5:3–12). Miller says that heaven is "filled with earth's broken lives."

What would motivate God to seek such material out of which to build His matchless and eternal kingdom? We know that God is love and that everything He does is motivated by His consummate love. But that truth is only part of the answer to the question. The greater truth is that He has no other possibilities. If He is to build a kingdom, fill a church, or populate heaven with humans, He only has failures with which to work. The Bible clearly asserts that we are all, every one of us, down to the last person, broken, wounded, and self-centered sinners.

We should not be surprised to realize that all God has to work with are sinners. The Bible is filled with that declaration. For example, Isaiah 53:6 affirms, "We all like sheep have gone astray. We have turned each of us toward our own way." Psalm 14:3 (ESV) declares, "All have turned aside, they have together become corrupt; There is no one who does good, not even one." Jesus Himself tells us, "No one is good––except God alone" (Luke 18:19). Paul, who called himself the "chief of sinners" (1 Timothy 1:15), summed it up in Romans 3:23, "All have sinned and fallen short of the glory of God."

We remind ourselves of this truth not because we wish to beat ourselves (or others) up. I do myself no favor by condemning myself for my human weakness or my natural and built-in inclination to selfish thoughts and behavior. Neither do I help the other by using words like "depraved," "useless," or "beneath pity" to describe my measurement of his or her value., especially when I use these and similar words to describe how God sees the other person (or myself). But, by the same token, I help neither myself nor others by denying the truth. As Paul put it, I do fall short of the glory of God. I need that truth about me.

Anthony Bloom (1914–2002) was a Russian Orthodox priest born in Russia who escaped to England as a young man. He is the author of over thirty devotional and inspiring books. He described our need for the truth about ourselves like this. "What we must start with [...] is the certainty that we are sinners in need of salvation, that we are cut off from God and that we cannot live without him and that all we can offer God is our desperate longing to be made such that God can receive us, receive us in repentance, receive us in mercy and love." We need that truth, he goes on to add, because "God can save the sinner you are but not the saint you pretend to be."

To sin is to "fall short of God's glory." Both the Hebrew and Greek words translated in the Bible with the word "sin" is an archery term. To sin is to shoot the arrow toward the target but to miss it. Sin is not breaking a list of rules that God has arbitrarily drawn up for us to slavishly follow. God gives in the Bible His description of living life in the most exciting, enjoyable, and creative way.

In a sense, the Bible is like an "owner's manual" which comes with a new car. It is not a list of difficult and unnecessary rules which the owner is forced to obey. Rather, it instructs the owner how to properly care for the automobile to insure its long and enjoyable life. To fail to care for the car in that way is to "miss the target." And the owner will surely pay heavy consequences for his failure. So it is with life. To miss God's target is to miss the fullness and joy of life as God intended.

We should note that missing the mark often occurs simply because we are, by nature, self-centered, egoistic, and lazy. We want what we want when we want it. Most sin arises naturally from that motivation. "If it feels good, do it" is a mantra we easily follow. But sometimes, human beings deliberately turn away from God and willfully disobey His instructions. They disobey God because they want to disobey God. The biblical word for such behavior is "rebellion." Rebellion is a willful refusal of obedience. It is an open and stubborn resistance to God's instructions. It is an arrow shot, not at the target but in the opposite direction (see Exodus 3:21, Numbers 16:2, Luke 23:14, and 2 Thessalonians 2:17).

The Bible is a book based on reality. It accurately describes the basic nature of human beings. In us are urges that push us toward loving acts of caring and compassion. There is a side of us that desires to help and pull others through a tough situation. No one can deny the natural human tendency to do good. But there is a darker side, a side that urges us toward the very opposite of these virtues. That is the side that gets us into trouble, and no one can deny the reality of that side. We all have it.

But recognizing the reality of human nature, the Bible offers an unbelievable solution. Jesus came to tell us good news about ourselves and God. We are far from innocent. Jesus pulls no punches in this area. But this is the surprising part: God still loves us. He longs for communion with every single one of us. He forgives our sins, no matter the details. He forgives. In Colossians 2:14, Paul says, "Having blotted out the handwriting of ordinances that was against us…, he took it away, having nailed it to the cross." Our forgiveness and the cross of Jesus are linked in a mysterious way. Exactly how it is not spelled out in the Bible. All we know for sure is that His love, most eloquently depicted at Calvary, overcomes our sins. If we ask in repentance with commitment to Him, He forgives each and every time we "miss the mark." Hallelujah!

I Love to Tell the Story

I heard a story once in Jerusalem that befuddled me. An elderly rabbi sitting in a group of about twenty people related the story. His greying hair was disheveled under his kepa, his long side curls (called payot) twisted neatly in place, and his black beard reached down to his chest. He was a skinny, small man with delicate hands, and his voice was crisp and his mind quick and active. I will tell you the story and see what you think. He began:

Long ago, when the great rabbi, the Baal Shem Tov, saw misfortune threatening his people, he would go away to a certain part of the forest to meditate. There, he would build a fire, say a special prayer, and the miracle would be accomplished, and the people saved, and misfortune averted.

Later, when his disciple, the celebrated Preacher of Mezritch, had occasion for the same reason to intercede with heaven, he would go to the same place in the forest and say: "Master of the universe, listen. I do not know how to light a fire, but I know the prayer." Again, the miracle of delivery would occur.

Still, later, the great rabbi of Sasov, in order to save his people once more, would go into the forest and say, "I do not know how to light the fire, and I do not know the prayer. But I know the place must be sufficient." It was, and the miracle occurred.

Then it became my turn, and all I could do sitting in my armchair was to say to God, "I am unable to light the fire, and I do not know the prayer, and I cannot even find the place in the forest. But God, I can tell the story. And this must be sufficient.

And it was!

I was the only gentile in the group, and the story left me cold. I was puzzled. The story seemed meaningless to me. But the Jews in the room were excited and pleased. They applauded and waited for the rabbi to go on with his lesson.

He did. The great and brave rabbi who first led the people to safety is Moses. He led them across the Red Sea, through the wilderness, to the safety of the Promised Land. Others have followed him with less and less success. Now we are here, and we have a story that we can tell. It is God's great gift to us, he said, that we get to tell and retell the story. It is the whole story of Israel, Moses, and the lesser men who followed. And here is the point: according to the rabbi, today, we participate in those miraculous events by telling the story.

As I think about the meaning of the rabbi's tale, I remember the conclusion of C. S. Lewis's first science fiction novel called *Out of the Silent Planet*. Elwin Ransom, the main character, has returned from his harrowing yet blissful and glorious experiences on the planet Malacandra. In the last chapter, he is talking with a friend about these extraordinary experiences on this faraway planet. His friend urges him to share his story with others. Ransom refuses because, he reasons, no one would believe him. "No," his friend tells him, "you must tell the story anyway, whether or not your audience believes you. At least they will have *heard a story like yours.*"

The rabbis say, "God made humans because He loves stories." Stories are powerful in and of themselves. That is why we read stories to our children and not the telephone book. Stories touch us at the deepest point in our being. They teach, and we remember what they teach. Think of the difference between an academic, detailed book and a story. For example, you can read a book that argues carefully and convincingly that Jesus is God incarnate. How much do you remember when you have completed the book? But read the annunciation story in Luke 1:26–36. Ten short verses that present the entire narrative. The story communicates pictures, not ideas. We see what is happening rather than focusing on details and facts. The images that the story paints in our minds are never forgotten.

Jesus taught in stories. We call them parables. All I have to do to bring the story to your mind is say the first few words. For example, *"There was once a man who had two sons...."* You immediately fill in the rest of the story. Or, *"Once a man was traveling from Jerusalem to Jericho and he fell among thieves...."* What picture do you see when I repeat Jesus' words, *"When you do it unto another, you do it unto me?"* Or, can you fill in the rest of the story when I say, *"Simon, you will deny me three times...?"*

Even on those few occasions when His disciples asked Him to explain a parable, He did not give an essay of ideas. He simply offered more pictures by teaching the meaning of various symbols (see The Parable of the Sower in Matthew 13:1–23).

Truly, a picture is worth a thousand words. A story creates a picture, or a series of pictures, that delivers us to the center of our being and opens up reality more vividly than a whole chapter of ideas. That is why the entire Bible is a single story. It is the picture of God's unceasing effort to redeem humankind and of the human need for that redemption. It reveals God's unrelenting effort to bring about His original purpose in creation.

Also, the Bible is a collection of thousands of other stories designed to take us deeper into the character of God, the nature of human beings, and our need for God's redemption. Further, Jesus' life is recorded as a story intended to teach us who God is, how He demonstrates His love, our desperate need for that love, and what must be our appropriate response to that love. Surely, Jesus' story is The Story.

Kate Hankey was born to riches in an upper-class suburb of London in 1834. Her family were staunch believers and members of the evangelical wing of the Anglican Church. Filled with an overflowing love of God, Kate gave her life to spreading the story of Jesus to rich and poor alike. She worked tirelessly to start Bible study classes across London and into the countryside. Her influence was especially strong among the young, who, in turn, became zealous Christian workers.

In her thirties, Kate was stricken with a serious illness, and during her long and difficult recovery, she wrote two lengthy poems. The first was called "The Story Wanted," and the second was called "The Story Told." This second poem led her to write a wonderful hymn that is still sung across the Christian world. The last stanza contains these words: *I love to tell the story / for those who know it best / seem hungering and thirsting / to hear it like all the rest; / and when in scenes of glory / I sing a new, new song, / 'Twill be the old, old story / that I have loved so long.*[17]

It is the "story of Jesus and His love." We may not know the place in the forest, nor can we build a fire, and the prayers have slipped our minds, but we can tell the story!

---

[17] Hankey, Katherine. "I Love to Tell the Story." Hymn. 1866. Text by Katherine Hankey. Melody by William G. Fischer. Published 1869: Philadelphia. Methodist Episcopal Book Room.

· CHAPTER 7 ·

The Beauties and Wonders of the Way

The Bible's promise of "eternal life" refers to more than the *duration* of life. This marvelous term, repeated dozens of times in Scripture, has to do primarily with *quality* of life. John Eldredge calls it "life to the limit." Of course, it is "everlasting" or non-ending life. But it is much more. Corrie Ten Boom reminds us, "You know that eternal life does not begin when you go to heaven. It begins the moment you reach out to Jesus." That means that we begin to experience heaven, the quality of eternal life, here in this life. It is a foretaste of heaven on earth. Too many believers live unaware of this other-worldly experience that is available to them. Despite their faith in Jesus, they live a life that misses this wonderful blessing from the Father in heaven.

Heading Home

By faith Abraham, when called to go to a place he would later receive as his inheritance, obeyed and went, even though he did not know where he was going. By faith he made his home in the promised land and like a stranger in a foreign country; he lived in tents.... For he was looking forward to a city with foundations, whose architect and builder is God.

Hebrews 11:8–10 (ESV)

The big yellow school bus dropped me off at home each school day at about 4:00 p.m. My chores were to feed and water the animals (cows, pigs, horses, and chickens) and milk at least two cows. My mom and sister were busy getting supper and doing other household duties. My dad would get home about dark. It was always dusk, especially in the winter months, before I finished up at the barn.

I loved these afternoon chores. Tending the animals who depended on me, the smells of the barn, the physical exercise, and the sense of responsibility and accomplishment were a special delight to me. But the most distinct joy for me, and what I remember with the greatest sense of pleasure, was my walk from the barn to the house when my job was done. It was night, and the lights of the house were on. I knew supper would soon be on, and my family and I would be gathered around a table of laughter, kidding, and sometimes serious talk. I still see the image of that lighted house, a simple, unpainted, wood-frame farm structure on a gravel road in the woods of South Louisiana. Even now, that walk from the barn to the lighted house brings a sense of anticipation of what awaited me.

Those memories help me today to navigate the dark waters of the modern world. My memory is a kind of parable that gives me a vision of what my life is here on earth. As a Christian and as a member of God's family, I have "chores" to do. But the life that He calls me to live is not onerous. He created me to live the life to which He has called me. My talents, aptitudes, and desires fit the life He gives me to live. It is fulfilling even though it calls me to responsibility and hard work. But there is a sense of accomplishment and purpose that actually makes me happy. I admit that there have been tough spots, but He has always pulled me through. And, most meaningfully, I am heading home to a city the writer of Hebrews says is designed and built by God Himself.

I think that is exactly what the author of Hebrews is telling us about Abraham. He uses different concepts and words, but he is saying the same thing. First, he says that Abraham walked the paths to which God directed him even though he did not know where he was going. Life is like that for a Christian. We walk God's pathways, not ever knowing where exactly they lead. Who of us knows the future? Next, he lived in tents, the home of the sojourner who was always on the move. Nothing in this life is permanent or fixed except the things of God. Finally, Abraham had his eyes immovably set on an ultimate destiny. He was looking for a new city with solid foundations whose architect and builder was God Himself.

A strange Old Testament figure who preceded Abraham was a fellow named Enoch. His story is told in a single sentence. "Enoch walked with God; then he was no more, because God took him away" (Genesis 5:24, BSB). The rabbis tell an interesting story about Enoch. An angel had visited him, and Enoch had agreed to live a life that was close to God. In exchange for that commitment, Enoch had made three requests.

First, he wanted to know what the experience of death was like. As time went by, the angel granted that request. He was given insight into death by watching others die. Next, he asked to know what hell was like so as to be aware of the dangers that face those who do not walk with God. Again, as time passed, Enoch was given a vision of hell. Finally, he asked to see into paradise, and this, too, was granted. But Enoch, having seen into the splendors and delights of heaven, never came back to earth. The writer of Hebrews tells us that Enoch was transferred from this life to the other life "because God took him from one life to the other" (Hebrews 11:5).

I empathize with both Abraham and Enoch. Having done my chores, I headed home, and there was joy and anticipation in my step. It was not that the South Louisiana teenager found joy when he got home. The anticipated joys of home enlivened his steps along the way. Abraham was looking forward to his heavenly home, and that made the trip through his sojourn on earth lighter and filled his days, though troublesome, with joy and meaning. Home makes "heading home" both easier and more jubilant.

One writer, commenting on Enoch, said, "One day Enoch went out for his walk with God and he never came back." Walking with God along the way becomes so joyful that we simply wish never to turn back. There is an old Southern hymn by an unknown author entitled, "This world is not my home." This is not home because "I am only passing through." It has a catchy tune and is fun to sing. But the song has always troubled me. I'm always uncomfortable when I sing it, and now I know why. The song contains the words, "I don't feel at home in this world anymore."

I cannot truthfully say that. I love life. This world is God's beautiful and wonderful creation, and I, like that teenager, enjoy my experience in it. Even now, with all the limitations that age places on me, I still love and enjoy life. I like the challenges, even the tough places, that make me grit my teeth and trudge on God's side. I know I am heading home and that the joys of this life are but a foretaste of the delights of heaven. But I am not at all missing the pleasures of this world. Rather, I savor them. My life with Rachel, my children and their children, and my friends in my church all make the road home meaningful and full of delight.

Chapter 5 in Genesis, which contains the unique story of Enoch, is the written account of Adam's lineage. It records the length of each man's life and who their children were. When the writer comes to Enoch, he replaces the word "lived" with "walked with God." It is as if he wishes to emphasize that there is a difference between merely living and walking with God.

All Christians are headed home. But far too many are stumbling along, dispirited and fearful, with little or no sense of power or victory. Yet they cling to life with desperation. But walking the narrow way at the side of Jesus can be altogether different. We can step lightly, lovingly, and blissfully along the way as we head for the lights of home.

Sunday All Week Long

"There remains then a Sabbath-rest for all the people" (Hebrews 4:9).

On the seventh day, the day after creation had been completed, God "rested" from all His labors (Genesis 2:2–3). Old Testament scholars point out from their examination of the creation story that each of the first six days ended with the statement,

"There was morning, and there was evening." That is to say that each day had a clear beginning and a definite ending. However, no such statement is made about the seventh day. There is no mention of an evening for the seventh day. Both Jewish and Christian interpreters argue that, while all other days come to a conclusion, the day of God's rest has no ending.

Doubtless, the writer of Hebrews had this very fact in mind when he insisted that we are invited to enter a relationship with God that can be characterized as a "sabbath-rest." By the time he wrote his letter, thirty or forty years after the resurrection of Jesus, Christians had coined a single Greek word to communicate this concept. They spoke of *sabbatismos*. We can live every day of our lives in an effortless, peaceful, joyful dance with God. Because of Jesus and through Him, we can have a sabbath life every day.

We must be careful not to misunderstand this reality. This is not an endorsement of idleness, laziness, or sloth. Neither is it a call for self-indulgent and irresponsible living where one allows, assumes, or expects that someone else will perform the necessary tasks to ensure life's necessities. I once saw a televised interview with a young man who lived on a California beach. He had no job and had not worked for years. His needs were met by welfare, which supplied him with housing, clothes, and food. He spent his time doing what he loved most: surfing, doing drugs, and chasing girls. He was smug and very proud of the life he lived.

There is sadness about this young man and many in our society who are like him. He refuses to be what God has created him to be. Underneath the bravado and behind the satisfied smile that seemed to come easily across his face is a heart of fear. He fears that he cannot be what he really, fundamentally, is. The potential that is easily seen in his intelligence and street smarts is not being realized. He is refusing to be who he is, and that is not what the sabbath-rest is all about. His choices lead to despair, not peace and love.

When Jesus said that "the sabbath was made for man and not man for the sabbath" (Mark 2:27), He was insisting that God gave the sabbath to meet human needs. The sabbath is a day intended for spiritual, mental, and physical restoration. God gave the sabbath to mankind to make life fuller and better. To do the sabbath as God intended makes us better. It adds to our humanness.

The Lord's Day, as Christians call Sunday, is indeed a special day of rest and worship. We place our attention on God in a distinct way on that day of worship, fellowship, and rest. That is true, and we forget that truth at great peril. But an unexpected concept jumps out from the reference in Hebrews quoted at the head of this essay. The writer announces that we enter into a sabbath rest and can live there *every day of our lives!* Christians are not expected to be workers out in the world (seen as *profane* space) for five days and then turn our attention to God one day on the weekend (seen as *sacred* space). Sunday observance is important, but there is a great deal more to our faith than the one-day-a-week performance.

To live the sabbath-rest is to be busy and occupied with the practical affairs of life in a happy and cheerful affirmation of the reality of our own being. We acquiesce peacefully to God's will at the place where our life now stands. Simply put, while we constantly and continually seek to grow in our faith, we are not self-condemning. We love and accept ourselves and offer the gifts that God has given us (talents, aptitudes, desires) to God for His glory.

On numerous occasions, Paul referred to this concept as "Christ in you" (see Romans 8:10, Colossians 1:27, and Galatians 2:20). With Christ, we accept the life that we live. Our trust in Him brings peace no matter what events swirl around us. He promised peace to us even in the midst of the storm. He said, "My peace I give to you" (John 14:27, ESV). The sabbath-rest brings us respite and joy in God even in the troubles and challenges of life.

Isn't this exactly what Jesus promised when He said, "Come to me all you who are exhausted and carry a heavy burden and I will give you rest"? (Matthew 11:28). He invites us to put His "yoke" on our shoulders. Notice that He offers rest and, at the same time, incites us to place an instrument of work on ourselves. Are these mutually exclusive concepts? Not at all because His yoke "fits." There is an early legend that Jesus the carpenter made the most perfect yokes in all of Israel. He had a sign above the door to His shop in Nazareth that read, "My yoke fits!" We work restfully and at peace in His kingdom.

Sabbath-rest, it must be understood, is a spiritual and mental attitude. It arises from the inside and is not a result of external factors. It is not the result of "spare time," vacation, weekend, or a holiday. It is an attitude of mind, a condition of the soul. It is the peace that results from the reality, "God is with me." It is a state of inward calm. There have been times in my adult life when I have been so preoccupied with the work I was doing that I forgot all about time. The day was gone before I knew it. That is sabbath-rest. Years ago, when Rachel was still teaching and had more to do than she had time to do, she would pray, "Let my hands move fast, but let my heart be at rest." That is the attitude that brings sabbath-rest.

There is a certain mystery in sabbath-rest. Where exactly does the serenity, the peace that passes understanding, come from? How can we be busy with life and at the same time comfortable and at ease? How do we attain deep confidence and trust so that we can allow life to take its course? I remember the elderly Vermont farmer who was asked the secret of his longevity. He answered, "When it rains, I let it." Wow. How do we come to that kind of mentality in all of life?

The answer is simple but not easy. It is a gift from God that comes from the prayer, "Lord, teach me to trust you."

Longing for God

"The ox knows its owner, and the donkey its master's crib; but Israel does not know…" (Isaiah 1:3, NRSV).

The French writer Julien Green recently published an account of his conversion to Christianity. He tells how, in his youth, he was in bondage to "the pleasures of the flesh." He had no religious convictions to restrain him and easily and naturally, it seemed to him, led a profligate life. And yet, strange as it might seem, he often entered a church with a longing in his heart that he could not explain. It was as if he hoped that, by some miracle, he might instantly be set free. No miracle occurred, he reports, "but, from afar off," there was "the sense of a presence." He was aware that he desired this presence but did not know how to invite it closer.

Green spent years in that "in-between searching and longing" stage. He studied oriental religions. He even studied Hebrew to investigate Judaism. One day, he opened the Bible and began to read. His eye fell on the passage quoted above. Animals know their owner and their home stall. But, he realized he was like Israel, whom God was entreating to come home, and he had no idea where to go. He read day after day and came to know the stories of Jesus. He saw God in Jesus, having come to reach out to humankind to satisfy that longing for God and home. In Jesus, he recognized that presence that had prompted his search. In the truth of Scripture, he found the satisfaction of the longing of his soul.

The psalmist has a strange way of describing our longing for God. He says, "I will lift up my soul to thee, O God, in thee I trust" (Psalm 25:1). We have heard these and similar words so often that they no longer surprise us. They are a cliché, a commonplace statement that no longer grabs our attention. What does it mean to "lift up our soul" to God? What about "trust" enables us to "lift up" our souls? Exploring these questions can change this verse from a meaningless, hackneyed phrase to the beginning of something new and adventurous.

"Lifting up our soul" begins with the realization that, in Isaiah's words, "we are Israel." Isaiah compares humans to dumb animals. They know their place. They know where they belong, and they go there. A few years ago, when I lived in Missouri, I had a barn that had five stalls. I had five horses that I brought into the barn twice a day to feed. All I had to do was open the gate to turn them in from the pasture, and each one walked directly to his appointed stall. It always fascinated me that no one got out of place.

Even more astonishing is a report I read forty years ago. Texas Parks and Wildlife Department, along with their counterpart in Colorado, devised a plan by which they moved deer from Texas to Colorado. They did this to help balance the deer population in both states. The deer were tagged for identification purposes. Officials were surprised to discover that tagged deer began to reappear in South Texas. The deer seemed to have an inner radar that helped them satisfy a longing to return several hundred miles to their homes!

Julien Green's story of his turbulent youth and his fight to find relief offers an engaging image of the struggles that our entire age must face. "Lifting up our soul" means that we must seek our fulfillment in ways that are counter to our culture. We live today in a global culture in which there is a universally accepted way of life that seeks to abolish the awareness of God. God is no longer necessary in a world of science. Religion, rather than an avenue to health and well-being, is regarded as a debilitating disease that stands in need of a cure. The promise is that if we rid the world of religious superstition, we will set ourselves free. The opposite is true. Ridding the world of Christianity enslaves us in the hopeless world of the young Julien Green.

Despite the obvious chaotic consequences that a godless world brings (the breakdown of the family, lawless living, poverty, hate, abortion, unnatural sexual desires, transgenderism, transhumanism, etc.), the longing for that "presence" Green spoke of remains. It is of great significance that our deep desire for God is not extinguished even in a world from which God is banished. Frank W. Boreham, a British minister of the last century, said that the very desire for life is actually a longing for God. Perhaps he was quoting his British contemporary, G. K. Chesterton, who said, "Every knock on a brothel door is a search for God."

Blaise Pascal, a seventeenth-century philosopher and mathematician, described this longing as a "vacuum God has put in our heart." That is, it is a vacant space that exerts an inner pressure that pulls matter toward itself. Sooner or later, we acknowledge that we are the ox that does not know its owner. We have tried an endless list of things to fill that empty space. We try in many subtle and not-so-subtle ways to decide what makes us happy. We can be defiant in the desire to be "free" to determine the path we walk. We seek what we think will make us "happy." It was C. S. Lewis who said, "If I find in myself desires which nothing in this world can satisfy. The only logical explanation is that I was made for another world."

As Christians, we can come to know that "lifting up our soul" is getting down from that platform of pride. We "entrust" our life to the only One who can heal us and bring us to the place where we belong. His GPS and His alone lead us to the destination we all long for. Trust is the door that opens the path that leads to the fulfillment of our inner self. Paul speaks of that inner self when he reminds us, "The outward man is passing away while the inner man is being renewed day by day" (2 Corinthians 4:16).

When we "trust and lift up," we go inside. It is interesting that we have intricate maps of the earth's surface and can guide ourselves electronically from one geographical spot to another. We also know how to "climb the ladder to success" in the economic world we inhabit. We know the world in which the outer man lives and can make our way without a stumble in that environment. Yet, that world will pass away. But the world of the inner self, that part which is eternal, can remain forlorn and unknown, a land in which we are virtual strangers. We can be unaware that the discoveries to be made there are greater and more precious than those of the visible world.

The message of the Ecclesiastes is most necessary in this age. Solomon is decrying the effort to live life without God. "Try that," he repeats again and again, "and life degenerates into meaningless confusion." Nothing awaits life without God but loss and the forfeiture of meaning.

In Ecclesiastes 3:11, Solomon tells us why that is true. God has "placed eternity in the hearts of human beings." He has created each with a hunger, a longing for God. We can satisfy that longing. God has come searching for you because He longs for you. Can you believe it! Your longing for God is His longing for you! That is the happy news that Jesus came to tell us.

Living Easter Every Day

"Because I live, you will live also" (John 14:19, NASB).

An important question for all persons, Christian or otherwise, is, "Did Jesus really rise from the dead?" That is, did He really die on the cross on Friday afternoon? Was He taken down from the cross by two rich and influential men and laid in a tomb just before sundown? And did He come alive early Sunday morning to be seen in His resurrected form by up to 500 different people over the next fifty days? In other words, was this man heralded in His short lifetime as a prophet, a rabbi, the Son of God, the Messiah, and God Himself? Was He dead with no vital signs at all one day, and did He come back to life three days later? Much hinges on the answer to that question.

If the answer is "yes," if Jesus rose from the dead, it is a rational decision to accept all He said about Himself, about God, and about ourselves. We must take His way of living and His expectations for us in our way of life with utmost seriousness. Indeed, we are foolhardy to do otherwise. On the other hand, if our answer is "no," then why take note of anything that He said? His ideas are of no more value than any other human being or religious or philosophical system. One would be foolish even to consider Him a great moral teacher. Any man who laid claim to the kind of statements Jesus made about Himself, including the prophecy that He would rise from the dead, is either a charlatan or a lunatic if they are not true.

So, our answer to the question is of ultimate significance. What, then, do we say? I like the response of Lee Strobel. Strobel was a tough-minded journalist and atheist who set out to disprove the resurrection by examining the biblical and archeological evidence. His research convinced him of the opposite conclusion.

His 1998 book, *The Case for Christ*, tells the story. He says,

> ... I became a Christian because the evidence was so compelling that Jesus is the one-and-only Son of God who proved his divinity by rising from the dead. That meant following him was the only rational and logical step I could possibly take.

He carefully sets forward the ample evidence for the resurrection of Jesus (see 1 Corinthians 15:1–11 for a scriptural description of some of the evidence).

Stroble makes a lawyer's careful case with ample evidence. Chuck Colson responded to Stroble's study with a convincing argument. He said, "Watergate proves the resurrection for me." In the first century, he explained, twelve men testified that they had seen Jesus raised from the dead. Then, they spent forty years proclaiming that truth. No one ever denied it despite beating, torture, imprisonment, and death. Rational men do not die for that which they know is untrue. Colson goes on, "Watergate involved twelve of the most powerful men in the world, and they couldn't keep a lie for three weeks!"

Pinchas Lapide (died 1997) was an Orthodox Israeli scholar who argued in his 1982 book *The Resurrection of Jesus: A Jewish Perspective* that Jesus had been raised from the dead on the third day after His crucifixion. Among the many evidences that he found convincing for this fact was the following:

> Is it possible for deceivers or self-deceived to establish a faith that conquers half the world? In other words, can swindlers let themselves be tortured and persecuted in the name of an illusion—up to joyful martyrdom [...] Are there errors of a thousand years that are able to bring forth world-embracing institutions of faith?

His answer to his questions is no, and he concludes, while remaining true to his ancient religion, that Jesus' resurrection "must belong to God's plan of salvation."

So, the question of the historical reality of that first Easter is of decisive importance, and there is substantial evidence so that we can comfortably answer, "Yes, He literally rose from the dead." But there is another question of equal importance that we must confront. That question is, "What difference does Jesus' resurrection make in my life?" The message of Easter is that God's new world, His kingdom, and His new order have arrived. It is here, and you are now invited to live in it. This invitation is open to all His disciples everywhere. Jesus put it, "Take up your cross daily and follow me" (Luke 9:23, NLT).

One of the great contemporary New Testament scholars is NT Wright. He said, "Our task in the present is to live like resurrection people in between Easter and the final day." If it is our conviction that Jesus actually got up and walked around, showed people the wounds in His hands and side, ate food, and continued to teach His disciples, if that is our testimony, it should make us "resurrection people." That is, our everyday life should be marked with the sign of His living presence in us. Paul said, "I no longer live (that is, I died) but Christ lives (that is, the resurrected Christ) lives in me" (Galatians 2:20).[18]

Watchman Nee was a man who lived his life as "a resurrection person." Born in 1903 in a Christian home in northern China, Watchman's Chinese name was Shu-tsu, which means "the sound of the watchman's warning." When he became a Christian at seventeen, he changed his first name to Watchman. Life was hard because all of China was backward and suffered extreme poverty.

After the Communist takeover in 1949, he, along with thousands of other Christians, lived under the brutal persecution

---

18 Comments within parenthesis added by the author.

of the Communist regime. In 1957, the Party had enough of Watchman, and he was arrested and imprisoned because of his Christian faith. He was accused of sedition, and, refusing to recant his faith, he suffered vicious torture, solitary confinement for months on end, and denial of medical attention. He died after fifteen years of imprisonment in 1972.

What kept him going through a lifetime of struggle because of his dedication to Jesus? He explained it very simply. He clung to Romans 6:4–5, "Just as Christ was raised from the dead through the glory of the Father, we too may live a new life. If we have been united with him in his death, we will certainly be united with him in his resurrection." He said, "Our old history died on the cross; our new history began with the resurrection." Watchman Nee lived a triumphant life. He wrote many books about Christianity. He founded churches, schools, and homes for the poor. He preached about Jesus wherever he went. Jailers and fellow prisoners became Christians because of his influence in chains. He was a Chinese Apostle Paul because of Jesus' sacrifice on Calvary and His resurrection from the grave. Watchman Nee lived Easter every day!

None of us has faced the privations that Watchman Nee and millions of others have faced for Jesus. I pray we never do. But we face trying situations in living, sometimes dire situations. Each of us can live through whatever life brings to us if we live as "resurrection people." Jesus said. "Because I live, you can also live." We can live Easter every day. It is a life of power, accomplishment, and joy. He will help us if we ask. He promised it, and He will do it!

The Positive Effects of Failure

The story I am about to relate to you happened when I was in the eighth grade. I am not proud of it, but I am happy that it happened because it was a pivotal event in my adolescence. I started school when I was five, which meant that I was smaller than other children in my grade. I was often the brunt of jokes and almost always the last chosen for recess games. I developed a chip on my shoulder. By the fifth grade, the size difference was gone, and while it was not characteristic of me, I sometimes took out my frustrations on other children. Then came the crucial event.

The bell rang, and we were leaving one classroom and moving to another. I was among the last to leave, and just ahead of me was a boy much smaller than me. I was giving him the "zip." That is, I was grabbing between my fingers a tiny amount of his hair on his neck and jerking it painfully up. He reacted by trying to twist away from me and dropped his books. When he bent over to retrieve his books, I kneed him, almost causing him to fall. Suddenly, I felt a hand on my shoulder. Turning around, I found myself looking into the face of Mr. Hutchinson. He said only four words: "I'm ashamed of you."

To understand the gravity of this situation for me, I must tell you who Mr. Hutchinson was. He was a new teacher hired to begin a vocational agriculture program at our high school. A new building was nearing completion, which would house those studies. I was vitally interested in FFA and had signed up and been accepted into the program. Mr. Hutchinson had personally interviewed me and recommended my admission.

The spring semester was almost over, and I was to begin my studies with him in my freshman year. To have him aware of those negative qualities in me caused a deep sense of shame. What must he think of me?

I stressed over this dilemma for several days and came to a decision. Mr. Hutchinson, nor any other human, would ever see that kind of behavior from me again. I was not that kind of person, and I resolved to demonstrate behaviors and attitudes that would never bring me that level of shame again. I participated in the vocational agriculture program for all four years of high school with Mr. Hutchinson as my teacher. I won honors in FFA, and today, I list Mr. Hutchinson as one of three men who had the greatest impact on building my character.

I was reminded of this story while reading a news item on a new movement in the educational world. All of us know that children despise homework, tests, or the hours essential for study. All three are required not only for learning but for developing the self-discipline necessary for success in life. Beyond that, all three teach children that success is earned, not an automatic gift. Powerful educational leaders, however, deem success, self-discipline, and achievement to be another form of white supremacy. Academic rigor of any kind must be discarded as outdated symptoms of systemic racism.

This new and updated form of educational philosophy is known as "equitable grading." No child will be allowed to "fail," and to accomplish this goal, none will be allowed to excel. Homework will be assigned but not emphasized, and multiple "retakes" will be offered for tests. In some classes, there will be no tests at all. Class attendance, as well as classroom behavior, will not be a factor in determining the final grade. Supporters of this form of "education" note that student "hardships" will be given serious consideration that previous models overlook. According to *The Wall Street Journal*, several school districts nationwide have embraced the move toward this approach to teaching children. To make matters worse, this approach to teaching methods is gaining adoption in four-year colleges.

The rationale for these drastic changes in the education of our children is to reduce the "pressure-cooker" atmosphere of the classroom. It is designed to overcome the disadvantages that low-income children suffer and to remove the advantages that middle and upper-class children experience. One often hears terms like "leveling the playing field," "creating fairness," and "removing white privilege" in support of this approach. Proponents of equitable learning believe they are helping underprivileged children.

I see this movement as a direct attack on children of all strata. No child "feels better about himself" or grows in healthy self-esteem by receiving something that he knows that he does not deserve. The child may simply chalk it up to "beating the system" and "getting something for nothing." This kind of thinking may become a way of life for him.

No child grows in a healthy regard for himself and respect for others by being told that he is "wonderful," "exceptional," or "that he is a victim of the system" and that his lack of "rewards" is a result of powerful forces that are against him. A child grows with healthy self-esteem and respect for others by being given an age-appropriate task, being encouraged to accomplish the goal, and given praise when he does. He must be allowed to fail, and if he does, he must be supported and encouraged to try again. That, and only that, builds self-esteem. Even athletic events lose all interest if we know ahead of time that the score will be tied at the game's end, so no player may "feel bad about himself."

I have personally seen great improvement in performance in the college classroom by writing at the end of a failed test, "You are better than this! Get busy and show it!" That is almost always the truth about the student and is a compliment and encouragement to work to do better. Few people in our society today would be where they are if they had not been "forced" to develop the character and determination required to succeed. Besides, do you want a surgeon trained in "equitable grading" to place a stint in your heart? Or, what about a worker with that kind of training to build your new house or repair plumbing in your bathroom?

I thank God for what Mr. Hutchinson did for me. My behavior was unacceptable and deserved the shaming reproach he gave me. He sent my life off in a completely different direction. I made the decision never to give him, or any other person, any reason to repeat those words to me. He came to my house and helped me with my agricultural projects (pigs, chickens, and cows). He offered words of correction when I was moving in an incorrect direction, but he gave praise and encouragement when I did well. He lectured and gave tests and expected me to attend class and sit up and listen, as well as to do the homework he and other teachers gave. I did, and my life shows it!

Finding Philadelphia

"Make every effort to add to your faith [...] brotherly kindness" (2 Peter 1:5; 1:7, BSB).

Peter opens his second letter to the persecuted churches of the Roman Empire with the surprising admonition that they must "add to their faith." The entire New Testament teaches us that the foundation of the Christian life is faith. Hebrews 11:6 declares, "Without faith it is impossible to please God," and Paul teaches, "For by grace you are saved through faith" (Ephesians 2:8, BLB).

Faith that saves is a commitment, an entrustment, a surrender to God. That faith is radical and life-changing. But it is only a beginning. Peter is reminding these early Christians living in a hostile world that they should "bend every effort" to add to their initial faith. The beginning is trust in the promises of Jesus. We continue by trusting in the demands of Jesus. "Make every effort," Peter is saying, to learn the way of life to which Jesus calls us and to live your life from that perspective.

We may refer to Peter's teaching as a call for "moral progress." The image is of an advancing army steadily marching toward its objective. James Moffatt is often quoted as having said, "The Christian life must not be an initial spasm followed by as chronic inertia." We are not called to a moment of enthusiasm and wonder followed by a failure to live a life of continuous growth and progress. William Barclay says, "It is true that everything comes from faith; but a faith which does not lead to a new life is not faith at all." The apostle James puts it, "Faith without works is dead" (James 2:14).

After his appeal that his readers (including us) make every effort to add to their faith, Peter lists seven traits that Christians should endeavor to develop. We may call these traits the ladder of virtue (2 Peter 1:5–9). It is an impressive list that, if followed, will ensure that we are effective and productive in our experience of Jesus. Let us look carefully at the one listed next to last.

Peter says, "add to your faith 'brotherly kindness.'" The Christian attribute of simple kindness is sometimes (perhaps often) in short supply. Yet, it refers to a quality that is absolutely associated with healthy well-being in human society. Kindness describes a person who is hospitable, generous, warmhearted, helpful, courteous, thoughtful, and agreeable. One can readily see that it is very closely aligned with love. We can even say that kindness is loving a person more than they deserve. A person who is devoid of this quality can never be mentally or spiritually healthy, and a society in short supply of this quality can never produce healthy and happy people.

Aristotle once wrote, "It is the characteristic of a magnanimous man to ask no favors but to be ready to do a kindness to others." Jesus asked for personal favors only to catch the attention of others. He asked the Samaritan woman at Jacob's well for a drink, not because He was thirsty but to startle her that He, a Jewish man, would speak to a Samaritan woman (John 4:7). He took the lunch of a boy, not to satisfy His own hunger, but to feed over 5,000 people. Yet, He was everywhere and always kind in His treatment of others in need. He touched lepers. He wept with the bereaved. He defended the downtrodden. He ate with sinners. Virtually every page of the Gospels records a kindly deed He did for others, none of whom could repay Him. (Add your own name to those benefitted by Jesus who do not deserve it.)

Thus, the Christian faith calls us to kindness. Let us remember, as Scott Adams, the creator of the syndicated cartoon strip called "Dilbert," says, "There is no such thing as a small act of kindness. Every act creates a ripple effect with no logical end." Kind gestures heal. In fact, a kind act can reach a wound that nothing else can reach.

Jesus called "little things" big when He told His story of our final judgment in Matthew 25:31–46. He said, "You fed me when I was hungry, you gave a drink when I was thirsty, you invited me in when I was a stranger, you gave me clothes when I was naked, your nursed me when I was sick, and you visited me when I was in prison" (Matthew 25:35–36). "When, Lord, did we do these things for you?" we will ask. And He will answer, "When you did it for these little ones, you did it for me!"

What He recognizes as worthy accomplishments are such tiny things in comparison with the things we strive so hard to do. Once, He even said, "If anyone gives even a cup of cold water to one of these little ones because he is my disciple, I tell you he will certainly not lose his reward" (Mattew 10:42).

Bob Kerrey, Navy Seal, Governor of Nebraska, and US Senator, recognized how powerful kindness is in encouraging change. He wrote, "Unexpected kindness is the most powerful, least costly, and most underrated agent of human change." Jesus would concur. Every example of positive change told in the Gospels gives evidence of His use of kind and encouraging words. I think of His words to the woman taken in adultery. "I don't condemn you. Go and live a different life" (John 8:11). Or, the paralytic, "Take up your mat and walk" (John 5:8). And countless others to whom He spoke simple, straightforward, and encouraging words, and their whole lives were changed.

Words that communicate things such as, "I like you," "I see your struggle," "I respect you," "I know this is a tough place for you," "I believe in you," and "I am for you" are encouraging to the other person. As somebody who has practiced a helping profession for all of my professional life, I can attest to the powerful healing effect these ideas convey. A few times, the kindness conveyed in these words boomeranged on me, and no growth occurred. But personally, I would prefer to be gullible and taken advantage of than to be suspicious and tightfisted.

So, it is no wonder that Peter called for brotherly kindness. The word He used in Greek is *philadelphia*. That word, common in Peter's day, meant to be "kind as a brother." We extend an encouraging word or a helping hand to another because we ourselves struggle. We give kindness because we ourselves need kindness. And, best of all, in *philadelphia*, we are made kind, gentle, and warm-hearted by our gifts of kindness to another.

Why Pray?

"O you who hears prayer..." (Psalm 65:2, ESV).

One Sunday, not long ago, in a private conversation, Ed Wittel, a member of our Bible study, asked me an interesting question. "Why do we pray for things which God has already promised to give us?" he inquired. He gave examples. "Like, forgiveness. God has already forgiven us. Why pray for it? Or help. God has promised He would give us help in every situation. Why do we have to ask for it?" Raising his forearms with palms up in an enquiring gesture, he asked, "Why pray?"

That is a fair question. Christian faith is shot through with God's invitation to pray. It is a biblical teaching that it is both possible and desirable to address God and engage in conversation with Him. God is called "the one who hears prayers" (Psalm

65:2, CSB). Everywhere in Scripture, we are assured that God can and will respond to our prayers.

Prayer is a conversation with God. Paul said, "Pray without ceasing" (1 Thessalonians 5:17, ESV), an admonition that urges us to take a prayerful approach to our entire life. But the Bible clearly teaches that we engage with God in prayer using more than the words of our mouths. Psalm 19:14 says, "May the words of my mouth and the meditations of my heart be acceptable to you." Words are important, of course, but thoughts and mental pictures are important ways to pray.

Prayer may be a sacrificial gift, a dance, a song, a body position, a set of gestures, or pictures we create in our minds. We can pray sitting in silence. We can pray the Scriptures by selecting a passage and reading it slowly aloud, perhaps more than once. We can quietly picture ourselves as a participant in a biblical scene. It is worth noting at this point that the book of the Bible that most instructs us on praying and most encourages us to pray is called Psalms, a book of songs.

We must remember always that prayer is not a way of getting things from God. During the eleven months during which my father was dying with cancer of the brain, I spent every minute I could with him. I was living and working in Texas, and he was in South Louisiana. So, every long weekend and every holiday and vacation day, I made the trip to spend with him. Some of the happiest moments in my life were with him, sitting in his backyard and talking. During those visits, I cannot remember asking for a single thing from him. My only desire was to be with him, to learn as much about him as he was willing to tell, and let him know how much I loved him. I would take nothing for those happy hours in conversation with my dad.

For me, prayer with God is like those conversations with my dad. Only prayer is more. In prayer, we put ourselves in God's hands. We belong to Him in a deeper way than I belonged to my father. We listen to His voice and seek His guidance in an ultimate way. I am not reticent to ask for things that I think I need. I ask for the needs of others to be met in ways that seem appropriate to me. Yet, in all my requests, I am aware that the One to whom I am directing these requests is infinitely wiser and more compassionate than I am. It is the smart thing, I think, to say as I make these requests, "Your will be done."

Prayer, then, is a way of being with God. It is said that prayer does not change God; it changes the one praying. Prayer is not simply a talking mouth. It is also a listening ear. Or, more properly, it is a tender, loving heart seeking to enjoy and come to know God in a deeper, more committed way. It is not so different than the loving conversations between a man and his wife or two friends spending time together. The difference between those conversations and prayer is that we are not equal to God. But out of His desire to commune with us, God stoops to us. He puts Himself on our level. Prayer is one of God's greatest gifts to us.

But wait a minute, how about Ed Wittel's questions? Why ask for things God has already promised? Are we not wasting time trying to cross a bridge God has already crossed? Not at all. In the days since he asked me that question, I have put some time into thinking about it all. I think that there are at least three reasons we can and ought to ask for what God has already said is ours.

First, asking God to give us what we know He has already promised to give *makes God happy*. The New Testament approaches that subject in many ways. At His baptism, a voice came from heaven saying, "This is my son *in whom I am well pleased.*" The Father took pleasure in the obedience of the Son. We do not often think of God as happy, but we should. The Bible begins with a happy God. God surveyed each day's work and commented, "It is good."

One of my favorite pictures of Jesus is called "Jesus Laughing." Painted by an unknown artist, it catches Jesus with His head thrown back in full-throated, happy laughter. Does it not make a father happy when his child, no matter the age, spends time with him and even asks him for help? Why would we think our Heavenly Father is any less joyful with our conversations and our requests?

Second, *Jesus set the example.* Consider what is known as the Lord's Prayer. The disciples asked, "Teach us to pray" (Luke 11:1). "Pray like this," He said. He began with praise and adoration. Then, He said, ask for bread, for forgiveness, and to be delivered from temptations. Bread is for today, forgiveness is for yesterday, and deliverance is for tomorrow. Jesus teaches us to ask directly for past, present, and future needs. He said, "Let your prayers contain what you consider that you need." That is enough for me.

Third, making requests of God, even for things He has promised, helps me *remember who I am.* That I ask God for help, guidance, healing, forgiveness, strength, or courage for myself or others reminds me each day of my need for God. It gives me the opportunity to remember how God has cared for me in the past and fills my heart with humble gratitude. As I ask God to meet a need, I can simultaneously thank Him for the needs He has met in the past.

So, pray because prayer is an expression of our longing for what C. S. Lewis called "the far-off country." We were made for heaven and close communion with God, and prayer is a foretaste of that reality. Ask, and you will receive, Jesus promised. So, ask!

• CHAPTER 8 •

Nearing the Destination

Growing old is a reward for having walked the planet for many years. Each one who is blessed with a long life goes through the degenerative process associated with aging. We all lose physical and mental strength as time goes by. We may deny these changes or cover them up in many cosmetic ways, but they remain, and we can never deny them. Time goes by, and we grow nearer our destination. How is a Christian to respond to this inevitable truth?

Ernest Becker wrote a Pulitzer Prize-winning book entitled *The Denial of Death*. In it, he says that fear of death "haunts the human animal as nothing else." Primitive people, he points out, being more childlike, celebrate death because "they believe that death is the ultimate promotion, the final ritual elevation to a higher form of life." Alas, he notes, modern Westerners "have trouble believing this anymore," which makes the fear of death so prominent a part of our modern psychological makeup. (Interestingly, Becker was himself unknowingly dying from colon cancer even as he wrote the book. He died in 1974, only months after the publication of the book.)

How does a person of faith respond to such ideas? No one knows, not even Becker himself, what lies beyond death's door. If we knew, there would be no need for faith. How does faith help us navigate the issues that arise as we grow older and face the reality of our mortality? If there cannot be any final proof, is there at least rational and logical evidence for our journey through life bringing us to a living destination?

The Land Beyond Imagination

"Eye has not seen, nor ear heard what God has prepared for those who love him" (1 Corinthians 2:9).

Lately, I have been thinking a lot about heaven. Possibly, that is because I have been studying the Gospel according to John for the last several months. I have discovered that on nearly every page, John records Jesus teaching about "eternal life," or about Jesus promising "everlasting life" to believers, or Jesus' insistence that those who drink His water or eat His bread "will never die." Studying this book of the Bible inevitably turns one's mind to questions about heaven.

Or, more likely, my thoughts move to that subject because of my stage in life. Each day is another step toward what comes when my life on earth is done. And is it not natural that as the time to make a trip comes near, one's mind would turn to thoughts of what to expect at the journey's end?

One image that comes to mind as I contemplate heaven is an experience my mother had at age ninety-one, a couple of years before her death. Twice, she had experienced the loss of her vital signs, and the emergency workers had brought her back to life. She wanted no more of that. A deeply committed Christian and a life-long follower of Jesus, she was ready for death. She signed a "Do Not Resuscitate" order.

On this particular day, she simply stopped breathing, and her heart gave out. My sister, who was with her at the time, could not bear to follow my mother's instructions and called for the emergency ambulance. My mother's life signs were gone for about ten minutes before the emergency workers could revive her.

During the time she was "dead," my mother had an unusual experience. She saw herself at the entrance of a huge field covered with green grass. Several cows and calves grazed peacefully as she walked by. Ahead was a clear stream that looked ankle-deep. On the other side was an area covered with beautiful flowers of all kinds and all colors. A patch of trees lay beyond the field of flowers, and out of the line of trees stepped my father, who was her husband for forty-five years. He called to my mother, "Dessie, you have come too soon. We want you, but you must go back. We will welcome you at your time,"

"I love you, darling," my mother said before turning back. She felt discouraged because she was not allowed to join my father. But she willingly did as he suggested. Interestingly, my mother said that she felt as the occasion was occurring that it took about ten minutes.

Opinions vary among scholars concerning these so-called "near-death experiences." Thousands have been collected and studied carefully by knowledgeable persons in the field. I only know that what my mother related was a real experience for her and that I find great confidence in heaven as I think about her impressive story. I ask, is this what heaven will be like? Beauty, animals, trees, flowers, those we know and love, deep peacefulness and satisfaction? And all that unendingly in the presence of God?

The Bible actually tells us a lot about heaven. It is a *city*, a new Jerusalem, whose architect and builder is God (Hebrews 11:10, Revelation 21:2). It is not a human city of crowding, pollution, and crime. This is God's city: beautiful, serene, providing all that we need for life. Heaven is a country (Hebrews 11:16). This is the country of which New Jerusalem is the capital. It is described in detail in Revelation 21 and 22. There are rivers, mountains, trees, and flowers galore. This is where we live. There we have bodies (1 Corinthians 15:40–44). Our new bodies are like the resurrected body of Jesus and are free of blemish and imperfection. We rest (Revelation 14:13). We serve (Revelation 22:3). There are gold and precious stones (Revelation 21:18–22). Each gate of the city is a single giant pearl (Revelation 21:21).

We must exercise care in interpreting these images. Descriptions of heaven as a place of gold, crowns, harps, and many other physical items should be considered metaphors. We use a metaphor when we describe something unknown by referring to something familiar. They are symbolic and intended as an attempt to express the inexpressible. These metaphors say, "Heaven brings joy like the beautiful and meaningful things of the earth bring joy, only more so." Paul says in 1 Corinthians 2:9, "No eye has seen or ear heard what God has prepared for us." It is not that God cannot describe heaven. It is that our senses and our minds are incapable of comprehending it.

The promise of the Bible is that God will build a "new heaven and a new earth" (see, for example, Isaiah 65:17 and Revelation 21:1). There is some evidence in the Scriptures that these promises will be fulfilled by God's restoration and redeeming the present earth and heavens. Paul explicitly notes in Romans 8:18–23 that "creation was subjected to frustration" (Romans 8:20) by human sin and "groans, as in childbirth" (Romans 8:22) for the time "of its liberation from bondage and decay" (Romans 8:21).

Some scholars posit that this redeemed cosmos that God will create is the heaven that awaits us. God will fulfill His original purpose described in the opening chapters of Genesis. On this renewed earth under the renewed heavens, God will walk with us in beauty and in peaceful fellowship and love as He originally intended it. Anthony Hockema expresses it beautifully, "The kingdom of God does not mean merely the salvation of certain individuals or even a chosen group of people. It means the complete renewal of the entire cosmos culminating in a new heaven and a new earth." (We should note that John 3:16 literally says, "God so loved the cosmos....")

In heaven, God revokes the second law of thermodynamics. This is the "law of entropy." That is, everything deteriorates. Everything is on a path to destruction and decay. When God suspends this law, death is extinguished and is no more. This act opens the door to life that never ends. We see God as He is! (Revelation 22:4). The barrier between humans and God is broken forever. And all the other devastation caused by human sin is removed once and for all.

Heaven is no "one size fits all." The excitement of heaven is based on our differences. God made us as individuals with different interests, and we all bring that unique self to the eternity

He offers. He creates a special place in heaven to accommodate the song we each long to sing. Together, we create the beauty of heavenly harmony and unity.

A Living Hope for "Old-Timers"

"God is younger than anything else."
Augustine of Hippo

The most beloved scripture in the Bible might be Psalm 23. It carefully describes God's attention, protection, and provision as our shepherd throughout life. It omits nothing. God leads us like a flock into every area of our life, good and not-so-good. At our side, He takes each step we take. The psalm builds to a full crescendo and concludes with this assurance, "I will dwell in the house of the Lord forever" (Psalm 23:6, BSB). All this and heaven, too, as someone has said.

As I grow older, I revel in the way God has cared for me and my family through all these years. I can attest to the reality, the truthfulness, and the dependability of the first five verses of the psalm because God did what He promised. And I cling with stubborn, fierce, and determined hope to the promise made in verse six. I can trust those promises of never-ending life in His "house" forever because God did what He promised in verses one thru five. That is a huge blessing that comes with being an "old-timer."

Hope is an essential quality for a healthy and happy outlook on life. Those, at whatever age, who live without hope, who, for whatever reason, are hopeless, live a slavish life of drudgery that fills their days with an inescapable sadness. Not only does this life of no hope drain them psychologically, but studies have found that their physical life is impacted. They get sick more often, for longer periods of time, and they die sooner.

Mental health workers call this hopeless kind of life "a slow death of desperation." This kind of hopelessness, it turns out, is pervasive in our secular culture. It impacts both the young and the old. Isn't it strange that these days, when we place so much emphasis on happiness, we have so little of it in our society? At a time when we have so many "things" designed to make us happy, why is it that happiness eludes us so completely?

We can divide hope into two basic types. There is natural hope, the hope that is available to any human being, and there is supernatural or Christian hope, the hope that is available only to believers. Old-timers come up short on natural hope when compared to the young. Young people have a short past and a long future. They can plan far in advance and enjoy visions of success and accomplishment. The future calls to them, and in the mind of the young, awaits them with open arms. Dreams await fulfillment. For the young, youth itself is a cause of hope.

The reverse is frequently true for those who have been around a long time. We have a long past and a short future. The "not yet" turns into a "not ever," and we spend a lot of time remembering the past, both the positive and the not-so-positive. Since we have so little future, compared to the length of the past, we turn from the "what will be" to memories of what is "no more."

But for believers, that need not be the case. We have a supernatural hope in which the opposite is true. We can cling to Psalm 23:6 because Christian hope bestows believers a future that is distinct from the failing strength of natural hope. For the Christian, the past, no matter how long in years, is short when we consider an infinite future. We live patiently waiting for a "not yet" of such duration that it cannot be measured in time. Further, its quality is so mysterious that it is beyond our most remote imagination. As Paul put it, "No eye has seen, no ear heard, what God has prepared for those who love him" (1 Corinthians 2:9).

Jesus promised eternal life to those who commit their lives to Him. On the one hand, eternal life has no end. It is everlasting. It never ends. On the other hand, it is also life that is characteristic of heaven. That is, Jesus is promising that here in this life, we can experience a foretaste of heavenly joy, peace, and harmony. We live in that hope.

Isaiah spoke of that hope as elegantly as it can be pictured. After describing God as one who "does not grow tired or weary" (Isaiah 40:28, ISV), *he* notes that among humans, "even youths grow tired and weary and stumble and fall" (Isaiah 40:30). Then he declares, "But those who hope in the Lord will renew their strength. They will soar like eagles; they will run and not grow weary; they will walk and not be faint" (Isaiah 40:31).

We march toward a place of eternal youth. Augustine said God Himself is eternally young. There is an old Christian hymn we used to sing at church that contains the promise that we are going to a "land where we never grow old." We must never forget that Paul says that we begin that kind of life here on earth! He says, "Even though our outer man is decaying, yet our inner man is being renewed day by day" (2 Corinthians 4:16). Even as our physical body grows old and loses strength, even as our brain doesn't work as it once did and we cannot remember things, even as our balance is not what it once was, even then our inner man is being made new. Heaven comes to meet us here on earth!

To a desert people accustomed to dry, sandy land, Jesus said that the life He offers His followers begins now and is like a "spring of water, gushing up to eternal life" (John 4:14, NRSV). Peter referred to it as a "living hope... into an inheritance that can never perish, spoil, or fade" (1 Peter 1:3–4). Jesus said that He is preparing a place for us so that "where I am, there you will be also" (John 14:3, NRSV).

George Matheson was born in Scotland in 1842. He was blind by age seventeen, but despite this handicap, he became a successful and prominent Scottish minister. At twenty, he was engaged to a young woman who broke off the engagement because "she could not be married to a blind man all her life." Matheson wrote one of the most meaningful and beautiful Christian hymns out of that heart-breaking experience. The first line says, "O love that will not let me go, I rest my weary soul in thee."[19] Think about the power of that line. God's love will never let us go in this life or in the next. Therein lies our hope. Paul says that nothing on earth—life or death, angels or demons, present or future—nothing in all creation "will be able to separate us from the love of God which is in Christ Jesus" (Romans 8:38–39).

When I ponder these truths and the hope they offer, my mind turns to praise. How can I ever show my gratitude to Him

---

[19] Matheson, George. "O Love that Wilt Not Let Me Go." Published in 661 hymnals. 1882.

for all He has done and will do? Here's how I do it. On the one hand, I praise Him in my heart and in words. I say my thank you continuously and without pause. On the other hand, Matheson's second line in his hymn of love is, "I give thee back the life I owe." He created me, and He died for me. To thank Him, I give Him back the life He has given to me. I live for Him.

How to Get Down from a Desk

"A conscientious act is not insignificant."
A 7th-century Arabian poet

My problem was that God gave me what I asked for. In my young, or younger, years, this answered prayer seemed a blessing, and I reveled in it. But as those years began to slip away, it made my inner life and self-feelings, so important to emotional and spiritual well-being, much more difficult. Here is what happened.

When I was about thirty-two, I stopped one afternoon at a local hardware and lumber yard to buy a few building materials. I was on my way home from my job. I was a professor at a huge state university in North Texas, and I needed the materials for a project I was working on at the small farm where my wife and I lived.

The manager of the store seemed to be the only person there, and he was sitting on a desk in the middle of the store with his feet dangling about six inches above the floor. I knew he was a smoker because a cigarette drooped from his lips, and I knew he smoked a lot because his fingers and teeth were stained brown. He looked about fifty and had a big belly and really skinny arms and legs. As I approached, he got down from the desk. I should say he lunged down. Clumsily throwing his body forward, he dropped as if he were falling several feet. I was afraid that he would lose his balance and go sprawling on the floor. The picture of that event, which happened over fifty years ago, remains stamped on my memory to this day.

That is the day I prayed the prayer. Leaving the store and driving home, I asked God to help me to take care of my body over the years so that when I grew old, I would be able to use my body in an effective manner. I prayed that I would never be like the store manager whose body, it seemed to me, was a burden that he carried like a millstone about his neck.

God answered that prayer. I have always been a hard worker, both as a teacher and as a farmer. I have been careful with my diet (with Rachel's help) and engaged in ample exercise, and I have been blessed with good health. My body stayed strong well into my eighties. Sounds good, doesn't it? But there is a problem. I did not grow old slowly or even gradually. Of course, I knew that if you lived long enough, you got old, and your body did not function as it once did. I knew about loss of short-term memory, equilibrium problems, loss of muscle and strength, and all that. I knew it, but it seemed far away.

Robert Jordan once said, "At my age, if I say it, it's already an old saying." That is a sudden realization for some of us; it was for me. I realized that I would never have to replenish my drawer of socks. I would wear out before they did. I realized that I would have to give up driving before my eleven-year-old pickup would give out on me. No more suits to buy, or hats, or footwear, or ties. My supply would outlast me. What I have will "see me through."

One day, I realized that I was too old to fail. That thought, however, was not as comforting as one would suppose. It is true that I could never be a "failure," but it is equally true that I can do nothing to add to my "success." I have always been greatly motivated by my impression of how I look in the eyes of others (that is hard to admit). It is a character trait that has been a heavy burden to carry. But at the same time, it has motivated me always to give my best in every situation. I felt a little down with the hole left in me by its absence.

However, one must be careful while still breathing to brag about life. In an article written on the eve of his eightieth birthday, Joseph Epstein quoted a warning given by Solon to Croesus, the richest of men and the king of Lydia, "Never declare your good fortune until your last breath is drawn." Nonetheless, I must report that I have lived an enchanted life.

God had me born into a blue-collar, hardworking, rural family who early and often took me to church. Many years ago, at Thanksgiving, I wrote my parents a note of gratitude. "You taught me three things at an early age that have shaped my life," I said. "You taught me to work. You taught me to study the Bible, go to church, and tithe my money. And you taught me the value of education." We lived on a farm and shared life with cows, horses, chickens, and pigs. Everybody had chores both morning and night. We prayed before meals, read and talked about the Bible, tithed, and honored the Christian life. Both my parents encouraged study and education, and from the beginning, they talked about "getting a college education." My start in life could not have been better. Those were happy days.

But now I have come full circle. I am back in the hardware store with the manager whose body did not serve him well.

He and I are in the same boat (or, on the same desk, I should say). I would look very much like him if I had to get down. I am saddened with the losses and with how little I have left to give to God. I think of Gideon in the Old Testament. The Midianites had invaded Israel and held Gideon's people hostage in their own land. God came and, addressing Gideon as a "Mighty Hero," commissioned him to defeat the Midianite military machine.

"Me!" Gideon exclaimed. "My clan is the least in my tribe, and I am the least in my whole family. You have the wrong guy! That's me. The Midianites are powerful. They are all over us, and they take what they want. And facing them, in my eyes, I am the least of the least."

I think the bottom for me was the day that my aging body forced me to part with Jubilee. I now realize how much that horse supported my identity. I loved him for many reasons, but not least among them was that he supported my self-image of strength and capacity. He blocked my realization of aging. When he left me, I had nothing to put in his place. It is hard to rectify that. One does not simply will it away.

But I return to God's dealing with Gideon. God's words are not only comforting but also challenging. "Go out with the strength you have," God told him (Judges 6:14). I hear God saying to me, "Stop focusing on your losses and weakness. Be aware of your strength, even if it is diminishing." I can still study and learn, something I have always loved. I get to continue to write and to teach (thank God for my SS class). I can still love, respect, and support Rachel and our children. And, best of all, as God told Gideon, "I am with you." That is no small promise, especially when you have to get off a desk.

But If He Does Not

"Suffering ceases to be suffering the moment it finds a meaning."

Victor Frankl

St. Philip Neri was a Christian missionary in the city of Rome during the 1500s. He ministered to and lived among the poor, the sick, prostitutes, and other rejects of society. While he had a lively sense of humor and people generally liked him, as a young man, he did have one major fault. At times, he grew irascible and often erupted into sudden bursts of fiery temper. He was greatly shamed by these sudden episodes of anger. One day, he went to the chapel where, lying prone before a statue of Jesus, he begged God to relieve him of this burden. He left the chapel full of hope.

The first person he met was a friend who had always been serene and kind toward him. For the first time, the friend was critical and offensive to Philip. Immediately, Philip responded in rage and criticism at his friend. Walking away, Philip met a second friend who had always been a source of consolation and happiness. This friend, too, uncharacteristically, greeted him with criticism and faultfinding, and, without thinking, Philip responded with a fit of temper. Immediately, he was filled with shame.

Philip ran back to the chapel, once more falling on his face before the statue. "Why, O Lord? Did I not ask you to set me free of my anger?" And the Lord answered, "Yes, my dear child. And for this, I am multiplying your opportunities to learn and practice a quiet heart."

Philip Neri's experience teaches us an important lesson today. On the one hand, God gives the incentive and the power necessary for transformation. That is, the desire to change and the strength to do so come as a gift from Him. Truer words were never spoken than when Jesus said, "I am the vine, you are the branches. You can do nothing without me" (John 15:5, CSB). Any branch cut off from the vine withers and dies. That is true. But, on the other hand, it is also true that Jesus said, "Anyone who wants to come after me must [...] take up his cross and follow me" (Matthew 16:24–26). He provides the strength to follow Him. But it is we who must move our feet, and it is our shoulder that must bear the cross.

Speaking of our prayers for self-transformation, Anthony Bloom (a Russian Orthodox priest) comments: "Our minds must be formed, molded to the words, filled and harmonized with them. Our heart must accept them with complete conviction and express them with all the strength of which we are capable, and our will must take hold of them and transform them into action." Bloom is saying that both fervent prayer and courageous action are required. They are two sides of the same reality. We depend with all our heart on God for everything and throw our will and strength into making our prayers a reality.

The title standing at the beginning of this song of God comes from a powerful story in the Old Testament book of Daniel. The emperor of Babylon was King Nebuchadnezzar, who, in his vanity, had constructed a seventy-foot golden statue of himself and required all the city to bow before that statue when the trumpets sounded.

Despite being trained for three years to be part of the King's advisors, three young Jewish men refused to obey his edict.

Furious with rage, the king summoned them and threatened them with death in the furnace of fire if they persisted in their disobedience. They responded, "Our God is able to save us from the fire, O King. He will rescue us from your hand. But if he does not, we will not worship or serve the image of gold you have constructed!" (Daniel 3:17–18).

These young men had prayed that God would help them live according to God's instructions and "not to defile" themselves while in captivity in Babylon (Daniel 1:8). They knew the prohibition against worshiping idols recorded in Exodus 20:3–6. Also, they knew that God had the power to rescue them from the fire if He chose. But even if He did not save them, they would not break the commandment, even if it cost them their life. To me, this dedication and sacrificial courage is the epitome of "putting feet to your prayers."

In the field of athletics, there is a slogan that is true in many areas of life. It goes, "No pain, no gain." Muscles that are strained against a weight grow stronger. On the other hand, if allowed to take their ease and seldom, if ever, are put to the strain, muscles grow flabby and weak. Lungs that are pushed to support the runner to great distance grow larger and more efficient. If never pushed, they lose capacity and efficiency. Even our brain, God's most amazing creation, becomes lazy and forgetful if allowed no time for the hard work of learning. To our physical body, ease is disease. These physical principles are equally true in our spiritual life.

For example, prayer, which is a friendly and real conversation with God, makes us stronger and more efficient prayers. We come to the point that we hunger for prayer. And there is a peace and sense of confidence that we enjoy in God's presence. Our trust grows, and fear and anxiety diminish. But we must, like a tired runner, push through and keep going, even (or especially) when it is difficult. Trust, peace, and joy are easy when life is easy. But when life gets hard, we must will to keep going because that is when we get stronger. To stop weakening us.

I grew up hearing preachers say, "A lump of coal under pressure becomes a diamond." The meaning of this adage is that hard times turn our lump of coal into a "brilliant diamond." I have found that to be true. A few times when my life has gotten hard for me, my lump of coal didn't like it. Psalm 74:1 says, "Why have you rejected me, O God? Why does your anger smolder against the sheep of your pasture?" That was me. But somehow, the years have taught me the truth of Abraham Lincoln's wisdom. He said, "I prayed for patience, and God put me in places where I needed patience." I asked for transformation, and God gave me transforming experiences. And He still does.

Today, St. Philip is known as the apostle of laughter and the friend of sinners. He said, "Charity and humility should be the Christian's motto." He is remembered and honored for his affable spirit and his even and quiet temper. God answered Philip's prayer! But He did it in God's own way.

Praying Is Dangerous

> "...a meeting with God is always a moment of judgment for us.... To meet God face to face in prayer is a critical moment .... God is power, God is truth, God is purity."
>
> Anthony Bloom

Jesus once told a story that we call the Parable of the Unjust Judge. (It should be named the Parable of the Persistent Widow.) In the story, a woman calls on a judge for justice with an adversary. The judge ignored her request again and again, but she continued to pester him with her appeal for justice. Finally, the judge gave up. He muttered, "I will vindicate this widow, lest by her coming, she exhausts me" (Luke 18:5). Jesus concluded, "And will not God vindicate his own chosen ones even though he seems to take a long time?" (Luke 18:8).

Jesus is encouraging us not to lose heart when God does not meet our timelines. God has His own plans, but we are to keep praying no matter what. When I was in high school, Jesus' story of the persistent widow introduced me to a new word: "importunity." This word means, as I discovered, "persistence to the point of annoyance." Jesus' story is not meant to teach us about God's attitude toward us or our prayer. The judge in His story is a Roman judge. These judges used their position to line their pockets with bribes that the people gave them to court their favor. To the people to whom Jesus was speaking, these men were "robber judges." God is not like that.

Rather, Jesus is teaching us our place in prayer. He urges: keep at it. God is interested in what your heart desires. A century before Jesus told His story, a faithful Jew wrote, "For he is a God of justice who knows no favorites.... The prayer of the lowly person pierces the clouds, it does not rest till it reaches its goal, nor will it withdraw till the Highest responds...and affirms the right." We must remember never to be discouraged and lose heart. Rather, always be tenacious in prayer.

But we must never be flippant and take prayer for granted, as if, when we are ready, we can conjure up God, make our requests, and be on our way. We may never approach God in a cavalier, off-handed manner. In the quote that stands at the head of this essay, Anthony Bloom reminds us that prayer to a living God, especially one who loves us, is a serious matter.

We do not meet God in prayer and remain unchanged. The kind of prayer that Jesus taught can have a life-changing effect on us. Our prayer too often is, "Your will be changed." We must never forget that it is we who are changed in prayer.

Still, the sad fact is that, so many times, we approach prayer as a way to change God. If our words are religious enough, and if we can make ourselves believe (have faith) that God will listen to us, we can get Him to do what we want. We can control what God thinks and how He sees us and persuade Him to fulfill our self-centered desires. We misunderstand Jesus' parable and think that we can move God, even against His will, to give us what we have decided is best for us.

I know this kind of praying. There have been times when I so much wanted a specific outcome in a situation, and I was afraid that God would not give it to me. So, I begged Him to do it my way. I pleaded for God to give me what I wanted. I reasoned that no one else would be hurt if I got my way. For example, I never prayed that other people would lose so I could win a competition or honor (or so I thought!). In my way of thinking, this made my prayer acceptable. That is not prayer. It is a self-centered scheme to have our way.

Real prayer is dangerous because it is a mirror in which we see, not God's face, but our own. The mirror never lies. We cannot avoid the "wrinkles and warts." That kind of honesty naturally creates a crisis. Meeting a loving and forgiving God in prayer can invigorate a desire to be "better," more loving, more forgiving, more generous, and more prayerful. It can fill us with the longing to know God at a deeper and richer level.

It can be as if, in our conversation with God, something breaks through which we cannot resist and cannot control. One writer said that the power of prayer is like an "invasion of the unexpected." To say to God, "I surrender my life to you," is to open ourselves to the unknown. It was like that with Abraham. He put his faith in God's Word, and "he went out not knowing where he was going" (Hebrews 11:8). Prayer is not getting things from God; prayer is giving ourselves to God.

Jesus teaches us this commanding truth in the Garden of Gethsemane, where He waited for the high priests and soldiers to place Him under arrest. Luke 22:44 records that He prayed till drops of blood broke from His brow (a rare condition called hematidrosis caused by extreme anxiety). He was in agony, a Greek word describing a battle with sheer fear.

The pressures of the entire human race weighed on His shoulders. There is no scene like it in all of history. He pled, "Father, find another way. Don't make me drink this bitter cup." It was not the physical pain, although it would be enormous, that He dreaded. It was the hate, the rejection, and the glee in the eyes of the enemy that He wanted to avoid. He also knew that their rejection of Him would come with extreme consequences to them. That is also true today.

But His prayer did not end with the request to be relieved of the agony of the next day. He ended His conversation with the Father with the words, "Your will, not mine, be done." There is no helpless submission here. These words are not said by one battered into submission or frustrated by having no other choice.

Rather, these words from the mouth of Jesus are the voice of perfect trust. They were words of strength and courage. And they were not anxious words based on fear or doubt but were peaceful and poised. They were a response to the Father's love. And they were words of victory.

Jesus teaches us to pray, and He teaches us how to pray by praying. He shows us that there are two sides to prayer. On the one hand, prayer is dangerous. We enter the presence of the King from whom we hold nothing in secret. He knows all, and He expects all. Faith in Him is a commitment, a surrender, an entrusting of our very being into His hands.

Prayer brings heaven down to us. We enter the gates of heaven while our feet are still on the earth. Prayer brings us into a life that is fulfilling, satisfying, and joyful, even in the midst of the storms that life can bring. It opens to us the joy of living the life for which we were created. Like Jesus, we can commit ourselves to the Father as a response to the Father's love. And as a response to God's love, our dangerous praying brings victory!

The Race Track

Albert Pinkham Ryder (1847–1917) was a widely recognized American painter whose work still hangs in many American museums. He was known for his dark themes, which portrayed boats floundering on stormy oceans, dark nights with the moon shining through storm clouds, trees bending in the storm, people rushing to escape some disaster, and other pictures of human struggle. On a visit to Saratoga, Florida, home of a world-class race track, he heard of a local man who, having lost everything on a race, went out and committed suicide.

Ryder was inspired by this story to paint a picture that he called "The Race Track." It is a black and white portrait of a horse running on a race track clockwise (the opposite direction of a race). The rider, without a saddle or bridle, is hanging on while the horse is straining to run as fast as he can. The rider carries in his right hand, held above his head, what appears to be a harvesting scythe. The symbolism is apparent. Life is like a lonely race in which we all desperately face a pale horse carrying death as his rider. We race to escape death but to no avail. Somewhere in front of us, we will face, alone and without help, the end of our race. The pale horse speeds toward us, delivering that destiny.

The American adventurer Richard O'Connell, seeing the picture in an art gallery, wrote a poem entitled "Death on a Pale Horse." Only thirteen lines long, it is a pessimistic response to the artwork that emphasizes our fear of death. He calls the death speeding toward us "toxic," a "deep trance," and refers to it as a "widening gulf," which we approach with "terror." He concludes his poem: *"All must hazard all on the race on the clock, / behold the pale rider, / swinging his scythe, / in that twilight that comes to each one alone / when the one sure thing is to lose all you love."*

There is, of course, some truth to be found in O'Connell's poem. We will all die. We face that reality with some degree of reticence. When we come to that moment, we may have the good fortune to be surrounded by loved ones, but we all step through that door alone. But there is non-truth in the poem, as well. Not all of us face death with terror. Not all see death as an enemy, as unnatural, and as a pitfall we must avoid no matter the cost. Finally, and most important of all, not all of us see death as a moment when "we lose all we love."

About four years ago, I came face-to-face with the conviction that I was about to die. I had been hospitalized for a few days with an infection in my kidneys. I left the hospital with cleared-up kidneys but with severe blood pressure problems. Over the next few weeks, physicians had difficulty treating this problem. Medicines given to lower high blood pressure lowered it too much, while the reverse was true of treatment for low blood pressure.

One afternoon, I suddenly felt very faint and dizzy, and when I tested my blood pressure, I was extremely low. Rachel drove me to our physician's office. Since we had no appointment, they put us in an empty office to wait. I was sitting on the examination table, and Rachel was sitting about a foot away. I was extremely dizzy and lightheaded. I was aware that there was a darkness at the edge of my consciousness that seemed poised to overwhelm me. *I am going to die*, I thought. I was completely calm.

I wanted the last words Rachel heard from me to express my love for her. I said with an unquivering voice, "Thank you for being my wife. Your love is God's greatest gift to me. I will love you through eternity." The dizziness and faintness seemed to deepen. I felt ready for the darkness, and I expected simply to die and fall off the table. I was also fully aware that I was not afraid or worried. I was fully accepting.

Obviously, I did not die. My physician came in shortly and took care of the situation. But my awareness of how calm and unafraid, how ready and open I was for death, has remained with me. I have no knowledge of how others feel at this moment, but if this is what dying is like for a Christian, we have no reason to fear.

Leonardo da Vinci took an optimistic view of death when he said, "Just as a well-filled day gives joy to sleep, so does a well-spent life give joy to death." To be sure, every healthy person loves life and hopes it will be as long and joyous as possible. The person who uses life well, who seeks and takes advantage of opportunities to do good, who helps his fellow man along the way, who tries to live as Jesus wishes, that person can face death, not as destruction, but as a natural part of life.

This perspective can be seen even in the life of a person who dies at an early age. I do not wish to gloss over the great loss experienced by the loved ones of a child who faces death or the death of a young person who has barely begun to live. What meaning can be found in such a death? There is great mystery found here, and I am not qualified, nor is any other, to give a definitive answer to that question. One thing I can say, however, is that I have known individuals facing an early death and families of that person who have found meaning in that tragedy. For them, the meanings of longevity and accomplishment are not the same thing.

For death to have meaning, life must have meaning. That is the only way that death can be faced with courage and even joy. Albert Camus was a French philosopher and atheist. He gained celebrity status in the middle of the last century (he won the Pulitzer Prize for literature in 1944). He once wrote that there is no meaning in life *because* of death. In one of his books, he declared: "Because of death, human existence has no meaning. All the crimes which men can commit are nothing in comparison with that fundamental crime which is death." Camus could find meaning or purpose neither in death nor life because of his deep commitment to atheism.

For the unbeliever, death is both inevitable and absurd. To him, we cling to life from animalistic self-preservation and try to fend off death because it is a meaningless enemy. We try to hang on to life, not because it has some intrinsic purpose, but because something in our genes pushes us in that direction. Death can have no meaning or purpose since, according to the unbeliever's faith, life is meaningless. Human beings are just one more animal and no different from all the rest. When the race is done, so are we.

This pessimistic understanding of life and death is inevitable and cannot be avoided by the unbeliever. The unbeliever has, in effect, killed God or at least made Him irrelevant. With God banished, there is nothing left but death. So, the dominant philosophy of today is "Eat, drink, and be merry, for tomorrow you die."

Christians are committed to the proposition that God, as described in the Bible, is real. He is who has performed the miracles observable in the universe and the miracle of life itself. Also, He did the miracle, which is each one of us. He has not fashioned such a wonder only to let it all rot away and disappear like a dead piece of grass. Jesus promised that He is preparing a place for us, and one day, we will be with Him forever in that place (John 14:1–3. See also Psalm 23:6 and Job 19:25–27). We live our lives committed to that promise. Note that I did not say, "We believe." Today, "believe" has lost its New Testament meaning and means only "mental agreement." Christians are committed! That is, we base our life on that truth.

It is true that Christians, like all other humans, are moving toward our inevitable death. But, despite O'Connell's pessimistic poem, we do not face death alone. Since we are committed to Jesus, we take literally the promise of Psalm 23:4, "When I descend into the dark valley of the shadow of death, I will not be afraid, for thou art with me!" We live our lives committed to the One who made that promise. He is the One who made us because He wanted us. And He will not throw us away.

In the 17th century, the mathematician/philosopher Blaise Pascal wrote about what he called "the great wager." He points out that we believers are betting our lives that death is not the end. We wager that there is life after death. The atheist, on the other hand, bets his life there is nothing after death. He says that death is the end. Pascal notes that one of us will win the bet. If the atheist is right, believers have lost nothing. But the consequences are immense for the atheist if the believers are right! Also, he adds if the unbeliever is correct, he will not have the satisfaction of being there to say, "You see, I was right!" But we will!

One further thought. Even if there is nothing after death, I still want to live as a Christian. It gives a purpose and meaning for my life. It is more joyful than any other style of life I could imagine. It is, to my thinking, the most rational, logical, and sensible way to spend my years on this earth. I like Jesus, and I like being His follower no matter what is on the other side of the door of death. Being a Christian fills my life and makes me happy.

• EPILOGUE •

The Ship

What the captain said was: "If we're loaded by mid-afternoon, we will sail today. If not, we sail at first light in the morning."

I sat with my back to a stone wall, which some farmer had built ages ago. It was the first of several walls that formed a terrace that moved like giant steps up the side of a gentle hill behind me. Olive trees, grape vines, fig trees, and pomegranate bushes dug their roots into the rich soil of each terrace. Some earlier travelers had moved large smooth stones into place against the wall, providing a shady spot for passengers to wait for their ship to sail.

I watched as half-dressed laborers heaved the large wooden boxes from several oxcarts at the edge of the sea. Each box was placed carefully into a small boat, and when fully loaded, the boat was pulled by a lengthy rope to the ship, where the boxes were placed on deck. That excruciatingly slow process was being repeated time after time.

I knew what was in the boxes because most of the freight was mine. I am an exporter of dried fruits and nuts to Carthage in North Africa, to several ports in Asia Minor like Ephesus, to the imperial city of Rome, and to the far west ports of Spain. I travel with my goods by ship to each city and personally collect the money that local merchants pay for my goods. I then return home to Judea with a heart full of gratitude to the Lord for the good life I live. Twice a year, I make this round. This year, I was worried because we were a little late and were setting out after the beginning of the storm season. If only I could have gathered my merchandise a few weeks earlier, the trip would have been over before the weather on the Mediterranean turned sour. "God be with us," I prayed.

As I watched the slow, methodical work at the water's edge, my anxiety grew. Even a single day could make a difference in our safety, so I was eager to get the freight loaded, call up the few passengers who would make the trip with us, and be on our way. My mind was so focused that I failed to notice the man who sat down on the stone next to me. His slight groan, as if with bone soreness and weariness, called him to my attention.

Turning, I said, "Hello, my friend. Traveling today?" I spoke with hesitation. He was, after all, a stranger, and I did not want to offend him by being too forward. His expensive white robe covered a body that looked strong and healthy. I noticed a gold ring on his right hand, and his sandals looked strong and almost new. He appeared to be forty or fifty years of age. His overall appearance showed him to be well-to-do, but since he seemed to be traveling with no servants, I assumed that he was not extraordinarily rich.

"Do I know you?" he asked. His eyes were steady and left me still uncertain about my welcome into his world.

"No, I do not think we have ever met," I replied. I paused a moment and then added, "I was just being friendly."

He watched several beach birds flying small circles over the workers. The birds were hoping for a morsel that may have dropped from the workers' lunch. Finding nothing, they flew on toward other ships that were anchored in the harbor.

"Yes," he finally said, "I'm traveling on that ship they're loading." He nodded toward the ship loading my freight. "I can't wait to get out of here."

I wasn't sure I should continue the conversation, but I abruptly spat out, "Looking for some excitement in the bright lights of the big city?" I smiled as I said it. In my mind, it was just a small, manly joke. But really, it was a nervous effort to fill the silence.

I looked back at the ship. We would sail south toward Carthage, delivering a part of my goods to that city. In Carthage, a passenger or two might depart the ship, and maybe some other merchandise would be off-loaded. From there, we would sail directly north to Ephesus, where, again, part of our freight and a passenger or two would leave the ship.

We would then cross the Aegean, sail between Sicily and the bottommost part of Italy, and up the western coast of Italy to Rome. Finally, we would head directly west to Spain. There, our trip would be complete as the remainder of our freight and passengers would be unloaded. The ship would then be reloaded with Spanish animal hides to be delivered in the opposite order of our port cities. With the blessings of the Lord and no storms or other bad luck, I would be back here in this very harbor in five to six weeks.

My mind had gone on its own little reverie as I visualized the trip I had taken many times before. I turned again to the man next to me, who I knew would be a passenger on the ship with me. I wondered how far he would go. I said, "Are you traveling on business?"

"No." He pushed the word through tight lips. I remained silent as he stared away toward the horizon that stretched across the sea. Turning back to me, he continued, "I just need to get away, far away."

"So, a holiday," I offered, thinking my words would encourage him.

"Not really," he responded, seeming to loosen up a bit. "I'm just tired of working so hard and being told what to do and when to do it. Others seem to be in charge of my life. I think that has been true all my life. I hate authority, and what I want is freedom. Liberty, yes, liberty. That is what awaits me across those waters." His voice had risen, and his words had gotten hard as he spoke.

I felt surprised that he had been so self-revealing in a conversation that was intended, at least by me, to simply get us through the time. I realized that the man sitting next to me was in some kind of trouble. I breathed a prayer to God for words that might help him.

Not knowing where to start, I said, "Freedom, isn't that what we all seek?"

"I suppose," he said with a lighter tone. "But I think I need it in a special way."

"How is that?" I asked.

"Well, I think I have been dictated to all my life. Restraints and limitations are all I have ever known. I want to be like the birds. They fly wherever they wish without restraints." He pointed with a bony finger to the beach birds circling about, still looking for a bite to eat. "Or, take that ship. When the wind catches its sails, it can move any way its captain chooses. I want to be the captain of my life."

"I agree," I said slowly, "those birds look very free. Yet their very freedom comes because they live within the limitations God created for them."

"God!" he almost shouted, "don't mention God to me. He is the worst. Let me get totally away from Him."

I waited, giving him time to go where he wanted.

After a few moments, he continued, "Moses was our great leader and gave us the so-called commands of God. These were his ideas of how to live. Other groups have their own ideas. I don't claim to understand everything, but we do not have the right to force our ideas on them!"

Here, he paused and seemed to gather his thoughts. His eyes squinted, and he shook his head slightly from side to side. His voice got even quieter, and he said, "Then God added the other thing." He turned and looked at me, "He says we are to help our neighbor. Well, my problem with that is I don't know who is, and who is not, my neighbor. At this point, Moses' ideas seem unreasonable and unworkable. I refuse them!"

Again, he paused, and I waited. Quietly, I said, "The Torah says to love our neighbor." His voice was very soft, and his words slow and deliberate. "All neighbors do not deserve to be loved. Some neighbors deserve to die. How can God be so unfair?" He looked down at his feet and slowly shook his head. "That is my choice, and I am free to choose."

"You are right there, my friend," I responded softly, looking straight at him. "Before every individual, there stands an open choice, and it has to be so. Without choice, there can be no good, and without choice, there can be no love. Forced love is no love at all. Being good because we have no choice is not good at all. But we must remember that choices set us on a pathway, and pathways lead us to destinations."

He had turned to look at me. His eyes seemed to burn with a rigid disagreement. He was listening but not accepting what I was saying. I forged ahead. "God accepts our choices and allows us to continue toward the destiny to which our pathway leads. If we make a poor choice that leads to a destructive outcome, He may intervene to give us an opportunity to make a different choice. But He will never override our choice. He created us with that freedom. God's choice is that we obey His directive."

"Obedience!" His voice was tinged with bitterness, like he was saying a curse word. "Obedience," he repeated. "Don't you see? Anytime you start with authority, you end up with obedience. That's submission, control, and powerlessness. I want freedom. I demand freedom."

I kept my voice quiet and steady; I was still surprised that our conversation had dropped to such depth, "Do you not realize that obedience is exactly what makes us free? You and I are free to communicate so long as we obey the rules of conversation and the meaning of words and gestures, even voice inflections. If there were no rules of communication and everyone could make up rules as they personally desire, no communication would be possible. Obedience does not enslave us; it makes us free."

He remained silent but gave no sense of agreeing. I continued, "King David has taught us much about our purpose as humans when he encouraged us to sing, 'Lord, you have assigned me my portion and my cup. The boundary lines have fallen for me in pleasant places.'"

"I know that psalm," he said with slight irritation. "But what does it mean?"

"It means that God has built the exact fences we need. And we get to choose if we will live within those boundaries. If we so choose, the fences make us free. If not, our choice enslaves us. Birds fly because they obey the purposes for which they were created, and ships sail freely because of the same reasons."

He shook his head slowly from side to side. "Not for me, those ideas," he said almost in a whisper.

A bell was ringing in the harbor, signaling that the ship was loaded and the passengers could come aboard. We would set sail in a matter of minutes. I stood, bowed slightly in politeness, and said, "I am Elihu of Jerusalem. I sail on this ship all the way to Spain. May we go with God."

He stood and shook his head in the slightest bow and said, "I sail also all the way to Spain. God or whoever goes with us."

"And your name, my friend?" I asked.

"I am called Jonah," he responded.

Turning toward the water, I said, "Come, the ship is waiting."

Printed in the USA
CPSIA information can be obtained
at www.ICGtesting.com
LVHW050221190424
777825LV00007B/224